For Single
Mothers
Working
as Train
Conductors

RECEIVED
2018
SOUTHWEST BRANCH
NO LONGER PROPERTY OF
SEATTLE PUBLIC LIBRARY

D1040870

Winner of the
Iowa Prize
for Literary
Nonfiction

❦

For Single Mothers Working as Train Conductors

LAURA ESTHER WOLFSON

University of Iowa Press, Iowa City

University of Iowa Press, Iowa City 52242
Copyright © 2018 Laura Esther Wolfson
www.uipress.uiowa.edu
Printed in the United States of America

Text design by April Leidig

No part of this book may be reproduced or used in any form or
by any means without permission in writing from the publisher.
All reasonable steps have been taken to contact copyright holders
of material used in this book. The publisher would be pleased to
make suitable arrangements with any whom it has not been
possible to reach.

The University of Iowa Press is a member of Green Press Initiative
and is committed to preserving natural resources.

Printed on acid-free paper

Library of Congress Cataloging-in-Publication Data
Names: Wolfson, Laura Esther, author.
Title: For single mothers working as train conductors /
Laura Esther Wolfson.
Description: Iowa City : University Of Iowa Press, 2018. |
Series: The Iowa prize for literary nonfiction
Identifiers: LCCN 2017049195 | ISBN 978-1-60938-581-1 (paperback) |
ISBN 978-1-60938-582-8 (e-book)
Subjects: LCSH: Wolfson, Laura Esther. | Wolfson, Laura Esther.—
Knowledge—Languages. | Multilingual persons—Biography. |
Jewish women—United States—Biography. | Divorced women—
Biography. | Women authors—United States—Biography. |
BISAC: BIOGRAPHY & AUTOBIOGRAPHY / Personal Memoirs.
Classification: LCC PS3623.O588 Z46 2018 | DDC 814/.6 [B]—dc23
LC record available at https://lccn.loc.gov/2017049195

*For
my mother
and
my father*

Contents

For Single
Mothers
Working
as Train
Conductors

For Single Mothers Working as Train Conductors

WHEN I WAS a very young woman, I spent many months working and traveling in the Soviet Union. The end of the Cold War would soon take many people by surprise. I was far from my mother and from everyone else who mattered. In the Soviet hinterlands, I met a woman I'll call Nadezhda. She treated me like a daughter. She had none of her own. She clearly wished she did.

Reader, I married her son.

There was more to it than that, of course. I met the son first, and, in the usual way, he brought me home to meet his parents. And the son was actually delightful. When he spoke, he grew irresistible. Small children (there were many in his extended family) were especially susceptible to his charms. They would wrap themselves around his legs when he stood up from a chair to keep him from leaving.

Those months spent in another language, an experience both freeing and confining, the tectonic historical shifts I witnessed at close range—these things changed me. That the changes might fade with time was unthinkable. I needed a way to bring it all back home.

I was too big to wrap myself around his legs the way the children did.

I hopped over to the States to take care of some personal business, then circled back to Nadezhda, her son, and the rest of the family in those hinterlands I mentioned, which were in Soviet Georgia. Nadezhda had just become a grandmother by her other son, who was the younger by four years. The household now consisted of Nadezhda and her husband, the baby and its parents, the older son (my intended) and me.

Julia, the baby's mother, complained to me about what I could see for myself: the family did not welcome her. The pregnancy had been an accident, their second. I say *their* second, but both mistakes were of course seen as entirely hers.

This time, the second time, Julia had headed over to see the family straight from the obstetrician's office. Nadezhda told me this part; it happened before I came to stay. Her coat still on, Julia made her announcement: the doctor had said that a second abortion would forever disable her for childbearing. If she didn't have this child, she would never have one.

A wedding was cobbled together, with a dress, a white one, a popular model that was designed to conceal and to be let out as the big day approached.

That Julia had no father and a minimum of education only bolstered the family's view of her as a climber. It did not aid her case when, a few years on, late one night after a glass too many, or perhaps more, her mother let slip that the story about the irrevocable damage a second abortion would cause was something the two of them had cooked up together, without input from any specialist.

By then, of course, there was no going back. Is there ever?

None of this had any direct bearing on me. I flew in, as I always did back then, with enough birth control and other stuff—dental floss, contact lens solution—for my sojourn, a suitcase full of extra everything, just in case.

We planned to settle in the States, Nadezhda's older son and I, so late one afternoon, I repacked the suitcase (its contents now much diminished) for the trip to the West. Julia, in her uniform of bathrobe and slippers, leaned against the doorframe, watching. The baby was lodged on her hip; everyone else was out.

Her eyes locked onto a flattish, flesh-colored plastic box among the things strewn across the bed.

"Can you leave that with me?" she blurted, pointing to it. "You can get another one when you get back to America, can't you?"

Diaphragms were a rarity in the Soviet Union. And when they were available, they were not fitted by a doctor in the privacy of a medical office. Indeed, in a bare Soviet pharmacy I had once seen a diaphragm for sale—huge, like a baby bonnet—in a locked vitrine, unpackaged, exposed.

Julia seemed oddly familiar with the little box and oddly aware of what was concealed within it.

"It might not be your size," I said.

Her gaze did not waver from the object on the bed.

I was reduced to stating the obvious: "It's used."

Even as I spoke, I knew that none of this mattered; in the USSR in 1991, cast-off birth control was the best most women could hope for. To refuse her request would be mean-spirited.

"I'll boil it in the big soup pot," Julia said, with a nod toward the kitchen. "To sterilize it." She placed the child on the bed and it rapidly dozed off.

I dove into the suitcase after the remaining, unopened tubes of spermicide and, what the hell, while I was down there, I also found the white plastic refill plunger that screwed onto the tip of the tube; it was for inserting extra spermicide when you felt like going at it a second time, or a third—she could toss that into the soup pot too. I explained how all the items functioned together and how to grip the diaphragm so that it slid toward and then into, rather than becoming airborne, which might lead to a stain on our mother-in-law's fancy wallpaper.

Julia never had another child. Perhaps she actually used the diaphragm, and perhaps it actually worked. On the other hand, she could have had a dozen abortions, and I would never have known. (Nadezhda's best friend, a schoolteacher like her, married to a man who didn't like condoms—isn't that redundant?—had had thirty. That was enough unborn children, she noted sadly, to fill every seat in her classroom.)

I say that I would never have known because although Julia and I married into the same family, we would eventually lose touch. Sometimes I get updates from Nadezhda, who hears about Julia from the grandchild, now grown. That's how I know she stopped at one.

———————

During my stay, I watched Nadezhda steadily amassing maternal rights as Julia's dwindled proportionately. Nadezhda was very skilled at childcare and loving. She warmed bottles. She changed the diapers and washed them out by hand. She rocked the baby and sang lullabies. The child couldn't have asked for a better mother than her grandmother.

Julia withdrew. She stopped caring for her own child. No way could she compete. She was the wet nurse, nothing more, and that petered out soon enough.

A few years later, Julia and her husband moved into their own apartment. Nadezhda reported on the phone that the little girl categorically refused to go with her parents. She's staying here with us, she added, sounding pleased.

After we got off the phone, I said, "When we have our child, your mother will not come over here to raise it. We'll raise our own child."

My words were met with silence.

Good Lord, if I'd been that child, I'd have chosen Nadezhda, too. And Nadezhda still needed to sate her daughter-hunger, so it was an ideal match. Kind of. When the child got older, Nadezhda took her to school and picked her up each day and made friends with the other mothers. The child visited her parents a few weekends a month until they split.

The person who was supposed to be in charge had not been seen for some time. A group of aged functionaries announced that he would be replaced, owing to concerns about his health. *Swan Lake* was aired, over and over. The people understood what this meant.

A few months later, fifteen big-bellied men sat around a table, signing papers. At one minute to midnight on the last night of the year, the hammer-and-sickle flag came down. Pundits declared the breakup bloodless and deemed that a miracle. There was, they said, no historical precedent.

Women flooded across the border: Russian, Ukrainian, Moldovan, Georgian, and so on, heading to jobs in Cyprus, Germany, Israel, Dubai. They would send money home. Opportunities included babysitting, waitressing, and modeling, according to the agencies that placed them. Agencies that were run, for the most part, by burly men with Albanian passports.

We housesat, the husband and I; we sublet; we rented. We were students; we were employed; we were unemployed; we were underemployed; we were self-employed. With the passage of years, we stayed in larger and larger places.

Dignitaries met. Friendship was declared. Memoranda of understanding were signed. Commitments were made. Nuclear missiles would be dismantled, their components stored somewhere safe.

My knowledge of Russian was in demand. I traveled a lot, mostly within the United States, accompanying visiting dignitaries; sometimes to Russia, Ukraine, or Kazakhstan. Interpreters and translators of Russian had full employment, for a time.

A few people grew extremely rich. Most slid into poverty. A middle class emerged. Those who could now afford nice things were very pleased. Some people vacationed on islands in the Indian Ocean.

There was war in Ossetia. There was war in Abkhazia. There were wars in Chechnya. The war between Armenia and Azerbaijan was put on hold. The war in Transdniester was put on hold. The war in Tajikistan came to an end. There were probably other wars that didn't make the news.

———

Children? I kept on asking.

We were past thirty. Six years we'd been married. We had good jobs and a large apartment. Exactly what did we still need to do? Buy a crib? Diapers? Just what was missing?

The last time I asked, he said, "We would need to put it in twenty-four-hour day care."

This was puzzling on several counts. Why have a child if we weren't going to raise it ourselves? Why place it in an institution? And what on earth was twenty-four-hour day care?

I asked the last question first.

"Twenty-four-hour day care?" I repeated, trying to keep my voice steady. "Would that be seven days a week?"

"We could take it out on weekends, if we felt like it," he answered.

"They probably don't accept newborns," I said hopefully.

"We'd have to look into it," he said. "When the time comes."

———————

Many years later, deep into another marriage, I'm visiting my friend Katya in Philadelphia, where I lived at one time. Had she ever heard of twenty-four-hour day care, I ask, back when she was growing up in the USSR?

"Yes, I think so," she says, furrowing her brow in an effort to recall. "I believe it was for single mothers working as train conductors. So they would have a place to leave their children when they had to make long trips for work. You know, if there were no relatives nearby to help."

For single mothers working as train conductors. Leave it to the Soviets to make sure that particular corner of the social safety net did not get frayed. But I wasn't a train conductor; nor was I single; nor did we live in the Soviet Union.

———————

Nadezhda keeps on writing.

When her son and I separated, she lived in Russia still. She and I talked on the phone twice a year: on her birthday, which falls in January, and on mine, in August. Then, about a decade after the divorce, she broke the pattern, contacting me in the month of March to tell me, in the first email I'd ever received from her, that her son was bringing her and my ex-father-in-law over to the US to live. I had trouble imagining them here permanently—in fact, I could not fathom it. They had seemed so rooted where they were. But I toggled over from the Latin alphabet to Cyrillic and wrote, "I'm happy that the two of you will be close by."

"The decision to leave cannot have been easy," I continued, struggling over and over to hit the right key. "I'll help you adjust to life here in any way I can." I included all of my phone numbers: home, office, cell. I said other things too, but this is what I remember now.

We read what you wrote us and we wept, she replied.

———

For months, I heard nothing more. I concluded that they weren't coming.

On the night of my birthday, just before sleep rolled in, I noted that Nadezhda had missed the day: for the first time in many years, she hadn't called.

In the morning, a birthday email was waiting, sent off at 11:59 p.m.

"We've been in Philadelphia for three months," she wrote. They were living with her son, his new wife, and their baby.

The time stamp told me that she'd struggled with her conscience all day before finally resolving to write. That they'd been here for three months before I received word of their presence told me that something had prevented her from writing sooner. Whatever it was, she vanquished it, because soon we were corresponding regularly. But there were no phone calls.

Before she came here, when we spoke those two times a year, Nadezhda used to pass the receiver to any family members who happened to be around—her husband, nieces, various cousins, all of whom I'd known well, back in the day—so they could say hello. Now I understood that her son was simply unaware that she'd been speaking with me all those years, for, having stayed on in America after we parted, he was never in the room with her during those calls or even, for that matter, on the same continent. His ignorance of our contact required no great deception on her part; it was just a matter of not mentioning it to him, ever. Everyone else—the cousins, nieces, et cetera—must have known not to mention it to him, ever, either.

In a recent email sent from her new home in Philadelphia, Nadezhda wrote offhandedly, "I'm very busy with my new grandson. I'm responsible for him seven days a week, twenty-four hours a day."

These words, buried amid other news, nearly slid past me unremarked. But I did wonder why a grandmother would be responsible twenty-four hours out of the day. Even in a culture where grandmothers are actively recruited for childcare, that's a lot of hours. The words echoed, they echoed something from some fifteen years back.

I recalled the old, sad questions: Why have a child if you're not going to raise it yourself? And what is needed in order to have a child?

The realization boomeranged back with a tremendous delay: he had not been referring to an institution for single mothers working as train conductors.

Of course, by the time I grasped this, the matter no longer pressed. It was a missing jigsaw piece, nothing more — one that fit very neatly into a puzzle long since stored on a high shelf.

The Husband Method

🍂

WHEN I LEFT that marriage, various tactless people asked if our marriage had run aground on the shoals of cultural difference—had my American habits and culture and his Soviet ones clashed, ultimately proving incompatible? How I wanted to believe that the answer to this was no. After all, we were just two individuals, weren't we?

Just as I was reluctant to admit the role of cultural difference in our marriage and its demise, I was loath to recognize that marriage to Aleksandr (not his real name) might have helped me speak Russian better. That would diminish my credentials as a translator and simultaneous interpreter, reducing them to an offshoot of wifehood.

But of course Aleksandr was central to my grasp of Russian. There are certain foreign words you are just not likely to learn except as part of a domestic arrangement: pilot light, pantry, cilantro, duvet cover, curtain rod. Building on my college major in Russian language and literature, with its emphasis on *War and Peace*, and, in preparation for that, the instrumental case and verbs of motion (don't ask; I've got them memorized, but I can't explain), I learned from him entire terminologies related to electronics, car parts, and fly-fishing.

When we met in the USSR in 1987, I assumed, based on the occasional English word slipped jauntily into his speech, that he knew my language well and was just holding back to let me practice speaking Russian. And then one evening in his home-town of Tbilisi, Georgia, with separation looming as I prepared to return to my job on a cultural exchange project in Siberia, I spoke to him in English for the first time. As we started down the five flights of urine-scented stairs that led from his family's apartment to the street, I poured out my anguish.

"What happens now?" I asked. "Tomorrow I'll be thousands of miles away. When will we see each other again?"

I paused, certain that he had grasped every word.

He shot me a blank but feeling look that said, *I can tell you're very upset, and I can certainly guess what it's about, but I'm terribly sorry, I cannot respond to the particulars.* As we continued down the next four flights, I haltingly reiterated in Russian what had taken me just one flight to say in English. Now I knew that this business of expressing myself in another tongue was for real.

Aleksandr became my teacher, his Russian my model for how to speak the language. He was a skilled storyteller with won-derfully clear diction. I understood him easily when I still had difficulty with other Russian speakers. He spoke a vivid Russian, rich in comic images, retro Soviet hipster slang, and borrowings from Georgian, his second language. *Chalichnoy* was a Georgian-Russian hybrid word frequently on his lips that described the local knack for wheeling and dealing, acquiring the unobtain-able, knowing which palms to grease, and doing so with grace and wit. Another word of choice, more a sound, really, than a word, was *eef, eef,* an interjection employed mainly by men from the neighboring republic of Azerbaijan to express pleasure—or anticipation—at the sight of a well-endowed woman or the aroma of a good meal.

He didn't go out of his way to correct me when I made a mis-take, but simply incorporated the correct form into his response so that I absorbed it without effort. If I thought I might have coined a word without meaning to and then asked if it actually existed, he would grin and say, "Now it does!"

When we moved to the United States, he often stuck with my little niece and nephew at family gatherings, especially early on, when his English was still shaky. They furrowed their brows and struggled to make sense of his unusual syntax. When he read to them, they corrected his pronunciation with excruciating politeness.

Once, we faced off for a playful skirmish, my nephew on Aleksandr's back and my niece on mine.

"Charge!" bellowed the boy, aged four, bouncing up and down on Aleksandr's back.

"Charge!" he cried again, seizing Aleksandr's shoulders and shaking vigorously. "Charge!"

Aleksandr looked puzzled. "What is 'charge'?" he asked mildly, adjusting the little boy's weight.

In the US, we discovered that marriage conducted in a foreign language afforded certain advantages: we could stand at a shop counter discussing a prospective purchase without the vendor listening in and engage publicly in secret exchanges of all kinds. But at times we went too far. Looking daggers at each other in a public place, voices raised, did we really imagine that passersby would think we were tranquilly discussing some matter of minor concern?

Once, as a tense exchange unfolded between us in the subway, a man who looked anything but Slavic — he was black — sat next to us for several stops without giving any indication that he understood. Then he turned to us. "Oh, you speak Russian!" he said delightedly, and this he said in Russian that was nearly flawless. "I studied Russian when I was growing up in the Dominican Republic. Please let me practice with you."

Startled, we complied. Now I wonder if he inserted himself deliberately in order to play peacemaker.

And so the public bickering ceased until the end, when it became impossible to contain. And still, I sometimes turn to a shopping companion to discuss the merchandise in our secret language, only to realize that we do not have one. Russian became the language I spoke spontaneously when awakened from a sound sleep. After I left Aleksandr, I surprised myself and a few other people by suddenly speaking Russian in bed.

––––––––––

About three years into our marriage, we became engrossed in Eduard Limonov's Это я — Эдичка (*It's Me, Eddie*), a profanity-laced *roman à clef* set among down-and-out Russian immigrants in 1970s New York. Laughingly, we took to emulating the main character, cursing each other out in the foulest terms we could come up with—the book contained much that was altogether new to me, and for Aleksandr, seeing these words in print was a novelty, not to say a shock.

After several days of this, we'd had our fill. "Let's get it out of our systems!" Aleksandr suggested, and like golden retrievers shaking off the water after a swim, we swore with gusto for a few moments, and then returned to the loftier registers to which we were accustomed.

He learned English quickly. But for our nine-plus years together, most of it in the United States, we carried on our relationship in Russian, switching into English only for quintessentially American topics such as credit cards, MTV, and presidential primaries. Sticking with Russian for all those years suited us both. It eased his adjustment to life in the United States, giving him a piece of home to hold onto. It kept him articulate and at ease, as I had first known him on his home turf.

In later years, when speaking with me he would sometimes shift into English. First, he would pronounce my name without rolling the *r* in the Russian way as he usually did, tipping me off that a stream of English was going to follow. When he did this,

I almost felt that he was possessed by some alien being, and I fought the urge to call in an exorcist.

During our last months together, I was translating a book about Russian obscenities and slang for something called the Sexy Slang Series, put out by an imprint of Penguin (see also *Merde! The Real French You Were Never Taught at School*). *Dermo! The Real Russian Tolstoy Never Used* was the title. The author of *Dermo!* (a word that lies equidistant between "turd" and "shit" on the crudeness continuum) was a plainspoken émigré living in Brooklyn. He had boasted in the New York Russian-language press that he and Solzhenitsyn, alone among Russian-language authors living in America, were able to earn their living by their pens, and this he did by churning out skillfully plotted post-Soviet potboilers punctuated with hired killings and rough sex.

"It's a smutty book," he said when he called to propose what I would come to think of as Project Dirty Words. "I would rather have a man translate it, but the translator I wanted is busy with another book. You're the best I could do."

I took the job but decided that I would contact him frequently with queries about the filthiest terms in his manuscript. I would make him squirm.

The book, mostly in prose, also contained eight or ten obscene ditties by Pushkin and other towering nineteenth-century figures, as well as some anonymous snippets of off-color and scatological folklore. Each time I crafted a rhymed, metered English version of one of these, I would call Aleksandr at work to share my achievement, launching without preamble into the Russian, followed by my English rendition. Picking up the receiver, he would hear me gleefully reciting something like this:

> Kuda nam Vasha Pol'sha!
> Pizda nashay Yekateriny gorazdo bol'she!
>
> Catherine the Great had such a large twat,
> By comparison, Poland's the size of a gnat!

Meanwhile, I kept my vow to call the author regularly. One day, some months into the project, when Aleksandr's and my marital breakdown had grown too clear to ignore, I phoned my client. After a halting explanation of some coarse term, he sputtered, "Your husband's from over there, isn't he? Can't you ask him?"

"No," I said sadly, "I can't."

Uncharacteristically tactful, he said nothing. I daresay he was a veteran of several marriages himself.

———

Sometimes, long after a marriage is over, clarity comes about specific issues that sparked resentment. For years, you don't have a clue what it was you did, or you think that one thing was going on, and then discover—far too late, but perhaps knowing sooner would have made no difference—that the issue was something else entirely.

One of our problems had to do with garbage—but not in the way I initially imagined.

Aleksandr loved to fix small appliances. After he arrived in the United States, friends and family took to giving us broken gadgets too cheap to have commercially repaired. Soon we were the owners of some eleven tape recorders, four television sets, and three or four VCRs, all of which he swiftly got in working order. Some of these devices we put to use; some we gave away; some were stacked in closets, along with the remnants of others he'd cannibalized for parts.

The sidewalks of our Manhattan neighborhood were also a rich source of electronics. Neighbors set malfunctioning appliances out with the garbage, often in the original box, including fitted Styrofoam chunks and instruction manual, the cord coiled neatly alongside. Aleksandr was astonished at the things Americans jettisoned.

I was proud of his abilities, if amused by his strange hobby. And here, too, my college training served me well, for in those years I frequently recalled that while reading some of Aleksandr Solzhenitsyn's nonfiction works during my last semester before graduation, I had somewhere come across a comparison, now suddenly germane, of the Russian soul (deep, long-suffering) and the American national character. (Among Russians, it is a truth almost universally acknowledged that to pair the word "soul" with "American" would be a gross misapplication of the former, even if English "soul" has nothing approaching the unfathomable depths that characterize Russian *dusha*, a word redolent of spirit, inspiration, breath, and a host of other things mystical and profound.)

In the passage I recalled, the great man observed in Americans a tendency to discard possessions promiscuously, unlike Russians, he said, who fix and reuse every sort of item imaginable, extending the useful life of things practically out to infinity. I cannot cite the source, but if I'm not making it up (always a possibility, especially after thirty years), Solzhenitsyn specifically faulted Americans for tossing out their shoes rather than taking them to the cobbler to be resoled.

I was quite sure that *my* Aleksandr had never read even a page of Solzhenitsyn—first, because when he lived in the USSR, he didn't move in the daring and rarefied circles where Solzhenitsyn's writings were passed illicitly hand to hand in barely legible carbon copies (typed nine at a time, because some expert producer of these artisanal publications, known as samizdat, had figured out that a tenth layer would come out faint to the point of utter unreadability), and later on, in the US, because he just wasn't interested. This gap in his education notwithstanding, his way with electronics was for me emblematic of avoidance of endless, destructive cycles of acquisition and waste, and of the ingenuity and spiritual richness that can arise amidst deprivation, all of which Solzhenitsyn so admired in his fellow countrymen and probably also in himself.

"Would you like a Walkman?" my husband would hear me saying on the phone. "Aleksandr found it in the garbage and made it work." I would say this in English or in Russian, depending on who I was talking to—we knew almost as many Russian speakers in New York as English speakers.

I felt him seething. Why? I thought what he was doing was so admirable, required such skill. I'd never known anyone with his talent for bringing machines back from the dead.

I polled my Russian-speaking informants. *Musor*, Russian for "garbage," was a most unsavory word, one of them told me. Since so many people in the USSR were poor, it was the custom there to throw out only those items that were utterly revolting or unusable. In addition, this person said, *musor* was related to the Russian word *srat'* meaning "to shit" and its numerous colorful derivatives, such as *sral'nya*, or "shithouse," and so, to the Russian ear, Russian *musor* was far fouler than American "garbage." For a long time, I thought that Aleksandr was deeply offended to hear me saying that he was rooting around in the *musor*, when in fact he was doing something much, much cleaner.

Over the years, though, I've asked many other Russian-speakers about *musor* versus garbage, and I've encountered no one who agrees with this explanation, no one who finds *musor* more revolting than garbage or believes that the word partakes of the stench that rises off the semantic defecation field. Just that one person, whose identity is now lost to time.

Yet I remain irrationally attached to the garbage/*musor* duality. I believed it for so long, and I want language to be at the root of everything, because language is what I do. And so I've come full circle: where once I was loath to believe that language and cultural difference had any bearing on our problems, I see now that I sometimes overestimated their role.

Garbage is *musor* is garbage, all of it vile and evil-smelling. What happened was simply this: I shamed him—blindly, foolishly, inadvertently—in a way that transcended language.

Climbing
Montmartre

2.

I'M RECENTLY POST-OP, having just risen after over a month on my back, and nearly every day my steps turn toward Montmartre. I'm living in Paris for some months, while my boyfriend (I'll call him Tristan) does graduate work at one of the Universities of Paris. (There are about ten of them; they're numbered; he's at Number Four.)

From the end of our block you can see Sacré Coeur. "A hideous whitehead protruding from the highest point in Paris" is how one guidebook aimed at the backpacker segment of the market describes the aesthetically offending cathedral, pointing out that when you are on top of the hill with your back to it, not only is all of Paris spread out before you but also the *banlieux*, or suburbs, France's answer to the inner city, with concrete housing projects like immense gray tombstones that—again I'm quoting the guidebook from memory—were built to establish a safe distance between the immigrant working classes and the Parisian bourgeoisie.

I've just been diagnosed with a degenerative lung disease whose name I cannot remember, let alone pronounce. I'm reduced to placing a sticky note on the wall over my desk with the name printed across it in block letters. It runs to several lines. When I glance up from the screen it catches my eye, and I trust that with time, *lymphangioleiomyomatosis* will start to roll off my tongue.

Before this diagnosis, I thought nothing of hopping a flight to Siberia or Thailand if that was what my peripatetic livelihood required, but now I'm told that plane travel is contraindicated, as the pressurized air in the cabin can cause my lungs to collapse during landing, leading, as I already know, to a stabbing sensation in the chest, followed by an inability to breathe. Funny how our bodies have such an intense need for the substances that surround us in nature. Oxygen hunger makes the heart flutter, the muscles weak, the voice drop to an involuntary whisper.

Our temporary digs are in a third-floor walkup. When I returned from the hospital in a taxi, too weak to climb the stairs, Tristan, skinny as an adolescent but surprisingly muscular, carried me up in his arms, ignoring my protests. I bared my teeth and moved to nip his shoulder, the handiest line of attack. After a moment, though, I found the ride was not at all precarious, and my fighting spirit subsided.

"Am I very heavy?" I asked, after some moments had passed.

"Like a feather," he said, pausing to catch his breath. "A wet feather."

———————

Almost every day now, I descend these stairs and head toward Montmartre. I pass through the courtyard, usually empty except for the Portuguese concierge compulsively hosing down the cobblestones and, in the evening, a trench-coated man in his sixties grumbling through a blue haze about his wife, who turns him out of doors when he smokes.

I turn right, passing the bistro next door, called *Á l'Affiche* (Now Playing) and decorated with posters of Yul Brynner, Clark Gable, and Vivien Leigh. After that, the corner store, the kind of place that sells pot holders, athletic socks, and towel racks at prices so low they hint at child labor in countries just over the horizon, then past competing bakeries whose proprietors set out baguettes in the morning and chocolate truffles at evening rush hour, past the most famous couscous joint in town (a recent poll declares couscous the favorite food of a majority of the French, demonstrating vividly the extent to which Arab ways are now striking at the heart of French culture), numberless cafés, a bookstore, and the beginnings of the porn strip on the Rue Pigalle. (Poor Pigalle! A popular sculptor in his day, his name is now linked with streetwalkers and the trade in red patent leather zipper-covered dominatrix outfits, with which, as far as I know, he had absolutely no connection.)

Now I'm at the foot of the big hill, looking up, taking in its shops and narrow, zigzagging streets, preparing for the assault. The peculiarity of this will occur to me only after some time has passed: laid low by a lung ailment, I am pulled inexorably toward the highest hill in town, climbing it with the longest stride I can muster. But now I think instead of all the times over the past twenty years that I've found myself standing at this very spot. My visits to Montmartre mark off the decades with an irregular ticking.

I was eighteen the first time I came to Paris, and running away from home, though I didn't know it then. I have no recollection of coming to Montmartre that time, but now I'm sure I must have, because whenever I walk down a certain street leading from the bottom of the funicular to the metro, a street lined with fabric stores, I think of the friend who came to Paris with me on that trip.

For nearly twenty years, beginning that October when we came to Paris together, she was one of my closest friends. We were in London for two semesters. I was living with my parents; it was, in fact, more their study abroad year than mine. Tuition charges were waived for faculty children at the institution in London where my father was temporarily teaching, and so I was pulled out of college at the end of my freshman year and taken along.

Starting out from London, my friend and I took the ferry across the Channel (this was pre-Chunnel) and checked into a decaying Latin Quarter hotel for a week. (It's still there, still doing a brisk business, still decaying.) With my high school French, I stepped into the role of interpreter. I spent our time there in a state of pure joy, in love with language and with place. Future unheeded and past forgotten, I was conscious only of the light hitting the Seine, the buskers playing their repeating loop of Paganini and Bach warhorses for solo guitar, and the fact that when I dipped into my limited store of French words, people responded.

It's now over a year and a half since I last spoke to that friend; we had a falling-out. But when I walk down that narrow street lined with bolts of cloth for sale, I feel as if we've just talked, much as you may think momentarily on waking that someone long gone from your life has just paid you a brief visit, an impression that is merely a vestige of the night's dreaming.

Another time in Montmartre, a decade and a half after that first time, I was in Paris for a few months, working on my French. I rented a room from a fifty-something woman named Marie-Laure. She slept on the living room sofa, giving me her bed, and sometimes talked about an Italian she wished she'd married. She took me to a Beaujolais nouveau party (a sort of latter-day Parisian harvest festival). As we crossed the threshold, she whispered, "Don't tell them you're my boarder; they won't understand." She introduced me as her friend from America.

One morning while Marie-Laure slept, I took a shower. When I emerged at around eight, she raged at me for waking her. I apologized and, propelled by her voice at my back, fled down the stairs and then up the nearby hill, past the butcher and the *fromagier*, past windmills and boutiques not yet open for business, to the kitschiest café on the kitschiest square (later in the afternoon, painters in berets, yes, *berets*, would be seated before their easels, daubing likenesses of tourists), where I ordered hot chocolate and felt terribly alone.

Hours later, I descended, glancing at the hand-lettered notices of room rentals stapled to the telephone poles, preparing to be told to pack my bags and seek lodgings elsewhere. She greeted me as if nothing had happened.

I was freshly divorced from Aleksandr then, unmoored, and taking French classes in a bid for professional and financial security, a job opportunity that had presented itself at an international organization. But my newly upgraded French had thus far brought me little I could point to, except the ability to grasp nearly every word of my landlady's outburst.

Another scene from Montmartre. One year later I'm back, still upgrading my French, still working toward that goal of the secure job that requires perfect comprehension. My parents are visiting. I've booked them into a hotel not far from where I'm staying, which is again, by coincidence, near the foot of Montmartre.

My father was always an ace at finding his way around foreign cities. In London all those years before, when I ran away temporarily (pulled back from Paris with a formula consisting of two parts love and one part guilt, or maybe I've gotten the proportions reversed), I always tried to duck out of the apartment before he asked where I was going. If I was incautious enough to tell him, he would pull out *London A to Z*, with its pages and pages of minutely detailed maps, and explain which bus to take, where to disembark, the correct British pronunciation of the name of the neighborhood where I was headed, and what anarchist publisher or watercolorist had resided there during the interwar period.

But now, seated on a bench in front of Sacré Coeur, with Paris spread out before us (including those tomblike apartment buildings thrown up to house the proletariat), I see that my father, pushing eighty now, is not the navigator he once was. With the Eiffel Tower barely concealed behind a tree off to our right, he gestures 180 degrees behind us, behind Sacré Coeur, completely in the wrong direction, and says offhandedly, as if confirming something he already knows, "The Tower is behind us, right?"

I'm startled. "What tower?"

That was the last time I ascended Montmartre before my lung diagnosis.

———————

Recently out of the hospital, I was sitting across from my surgeon. Call her Chantal Bonmot. She looked to be just a few years my senior (but then, I always think I'm the youngest person in the room), with creamy, freckled skin, dark blue eyeliner, and glossy dark blond hair held back with a black velvet headband.

"Well," she said, leafing through the file on her desk, "the lab has sent us your biopsy results."

I waited.

"As we thought, you have lymphangioleiomyomatosis, LAM for short. It usually affects women in their thirties, and often presents with a collapsed lung."

I found a notepad and pen in my purse and started taking down her words in a jumble of English and French.

She waved a hand in my direction. "No need to write this down. We'll give you your records."

I kept writing. "How do you spell the name of the disease?"

My question went unanswered. "Does it have other symptoms?" I asked.

She thought for a moment. "Shortness of breath, collapsed lung, that's about it," she said.

I'd experienced both and had just undergone an operation to ward off further lung collapses on my left side. She said now that I could have the same surgery on the right, as a preventive measure. I tried to recall what commitments I had over the coming months, to see when I could spare the five weeks it would take to convalesce.

"Is that all?"

"Oh, and perhaps you'll need *une greffe de poumons.*"

An unfamiliar word reminded me that we were speaking French.

"*Greffe*? What's that?"

"It means you'll have to get a new pair of lungs," she said. I admired her ease in defining the word. I've spent enough time learning languages to know that most people are hopeless at explaining difficult words to foreigners.

"*Une greffe de poumons?*" I mastered my new word immediately, right down to the gender.

"Oh, really," she said, "it's no big deal. It wouldn't be for another fifteen or twenty years. And many women with this condition don't live long enough to need one."

"Twenty years!" My exclamation overlapped with her last words, nearly erasing them. "*Mais ça passe vite!*" (That goes by quickly!)

Twenty years was precisely the interval that had passed since I had first seen—and scaled—Montmartre.

I began those obsessive daily treks from our sublet over to Montmartre the week I was diagnosed. I went alone. The semester was ending, and Tristan had term papers to write. At his desk, surrounded by open volumes of Heidegger and Husserl, he looked small.

I came to love that tourist trap and to know it intimately. The house, marked with a plaque, where Erik Satie once rented a tiny room. (In that room, I read somewhere, there were dozens of tightly furled gray umbrellas and two pianos, one on top of the other, giving new meaning to the word "upright," although in my mind's eye, the one on top is, in fact, upside down, pedals waving gently overhead like the fronds of some giant houseplant.) A building on a small square where Picasso and Braque collaborated to invent Cubism. The house where Bizet composed *Carmen*.

Le Lapin Agile, a cabaret frequented by Picasso, Renoir, Utrillo, and others, its name painted on a sign over the door depicting a rabbit bounding out of a skillet. A pink house that's home to a restaurant called—what else?—*La Maison Rose*. The Montmartre Historical Museum, which grants equal space to a gruesome exhibit about a mass murder committed somewhere nearby in the mid-nineteenth century, complete with an artist's depiction of the event, and to the Paris Commune, that epoch-making uprising of the poor and oppressed that culminated in the establishment of a short-lived egalitarian governing committee headquartered in Montmartre. (The ugly white basilica of Sacré Coeur was built by the powers that be after the popular government was crushed and order reestablished, for the express purpose of driving home who was in charge.) A plaque outside a café, noting that in the fourteenth century the building housed the sole grocery store in all of Montmartre. Narrow, steep staircases that circumvent the switchbacks that cars must take. A mansion with a sign out front explaining that back when Montmartre was a rural retreat, this place was an asylum for those afflicted with nervous complaints and mental disorders.

But what intrigues me most about Montmartre is that in spite of daily, unceasing violation by tourists, the exhaust from their immense buses, their flashing cameras, the place maintains its dignity, with its Cubist, unexpected views of the city below caught between the buildings, and with its alleys that seem somehow soundproofed against the swarming hordes just half a block away. Often I take a circuitous route, instead of marching directly to the top of the hill, and I emerge around corners to glimpse those familiar windmills from surprising angles; the funicular from a promontory jutting out next to it about halfway up; steep, impossibly long flights of stairs slicing up and down the butte between closely spaced apartment buildings; tiny restaurants glowing red at the windows, talk spilling out the doors, each establishment its own private party; a mysterious shop, always shuttered, with a hand-lettered sign that reads *Le Toit du Monde* (The Roof of the World), as if little Montmartre aspires unselfconsciously to Himalayan heights.

It's impossible to spend too much time roaming this place. You can walk the length and breadth of this tiny patch of land, trace the same hairpin turns again and again, and find in them inspiration without end. How can so much picturesqueness and invisible wonder, so unplumbable, be packed into these small spaces? Scraps of time and history become trapped in the interstices of the alleys and buildings, and slowly they yield up their fragrance. There is a vastness here that is temporal rather than spatial. How can a person lead a normal life in this charmed place, go to work, sleep in on weekends, get herself to the post office and the dry cleaner, and still make the time and retain the capacity for wonder that such a place demands?

If only I could take some of those wisps of time that linger in the alleys and crevices of Montmartre and tack them on to the end of my life, whenever that may be, lengthening it even a bit. Hemingway called Paris a moveable feast, which, once visited, remains with a person for a lifetime. Not true: departure approaches, and I visit and revisit these places, trying to absorb them so I can carry them away with me, knowing that this is an enterprise doomed to failure.

Because I've spent months and months here, I will always be somewhat blasé when I'm near Montmartre, thinking with part of my mind of errands and quotidian tasks. Yet when I leave Paris, as I will soon, I'll miss Montmartre, miss it terribly. I experience the place through differing degrees of absence, yearning, the inability to be fully present.

Proust at Rush Hour

❧

MY JOB IS A DRAG—like most nine-to-five gigs, I imagine. But, oh, the commute! The commute is a golden border at the beginning and end of each workday that sheds some of its shimmer onto the leaden expanse in between.

I'm a New Yorker, so taking the subway to work is a given. The subway provides, in miniature, all the charms of long-distance train travel, minus the view. There is the unencumbered time, a commodity beyond price for those who sell their waking hours in order to afford a place to sleep. There is the heady state of in-betweenness, a brief release from all worldly entanglement. There is the fact that subway travel is, for now at least, incompatible with email and cell phones, and that it will always be incompatible with vacuuming, dishes, and laundry. There are about half a dozen things, tops, that you can do on the subway: doze, observe the people around you, listen to music, read, think—things we should all do more often.

I was not always a commuter. I used to be self-employed. I worked from home, and when I traveled, my conveyance of choice was the jet plane. State banquets at the Kremlin, mafia trials, forgotten literary masterpieces, KGB files declassified under Yeltsin (later to be reclassified under Putin)—I translated them all. It was a halcyon time. The border between working and not working was porous: when work was slow, I took a walk or a yoga class;

when a deadline loomed, I worked weekends or evenings. As to why people dreaded Monday and thanked God it was Friday, I lacked all understanding. When people spoke of their commutes, I listened as to an account of some quaint foreign ritual.

But in my mid-thirties, panic bore down. My health insurance coverage was patchy, my retirement savings meager. My income blossomed and shriveled with the seasons.

I began planning for the transition from free spirit to commuter, boning up on my French so as to get that job I'd set my sights on. Apart from the expense, there was nothing onerous in this: who would object to spending some months in Paris immersed in the language of Molière and Serge Gainsbourg? This was a dream I had nurtured and then set aside almost twenty years before, and I was glad of any pretext to make it come true at last.

French mastered, I prepared to take up my new job as an interpreter of Russian and French into English, working in a tall building of green glass at midtown Manhattan's watery eastern edge. And now unforeseen things began to happen. During the trial period before the job was to become permanent, my newly failing lungs made it difficult, then impossible, for me to perform that demanding work. A seemingly firm job offer went limp.

Through a series of short contracts within the Organization, I tumbled down and down in status and job satisfaction (though not salary) until I landed in a permanent position editing English-language documents, with duties that called for no more than a passing knowledge of French or any other foreign language. Movement up the hierarchy, I would come to understand, was the reward for a different sort of fluency altogether, directly proportionate to the climber's ability to say nothing and offend no one, in the most elegant way possible, all at great length. Shortly after I started the permanent job, I was copied on an email from one higher-up to another (its contents presumably affecting my future in some way) that embodied this style so utterly that I would be remiss if I did not reproduce it here. "While I do not think that your concern is misplaced," ran this missive,

> I would say that it may be premature to suggest that the guidelines would apply uniformly, as they stand, to all staff. I hope I am not being overly sanguine about this, but I tend to think that just as our specificities are being taken into account to a large extent in the interim, they would readily be accommodated in the long term. In other words, the guidelines only state the policy, which will no doubt allow for some special dispensation. However, I do not dispute for a second that yours is a legitimate concern.

But, I reminded myself as I printed out the email and taped it to the wall over my computer between a map of the Economic Community of West African States and another of the former Yugoslav Republic of Macedonia, I was lucky. At last I had a permanent job. It came with health insurance, which saved me thousands each month on crucial prescriptions, medical equipment rentals, and doctor visits; disability benefits if I became unable to work, a possibility I now had to entertain; dental coverage so dazzling that even the receptionist at the dentist's office was impressed; liberal sick leave, of which I would take full advantage; a sun-splashed office with a view of boats chugging up and down the East River; access to a post office, bank, credit union, employee-only low-interest mortgages, medical service, international newsstand, yoga, dancercise, and Pilates classes, a cappuccino bar, cafeteria, fancy restaurant with enormous bowls of whipped cream and raspberries on the all-you-can-eat dessert buffet, nine levels of instruction, at no cost, in my choice of Spanish, Arabic, or Mandarin, and high school choirs visiting from the heartland singing songs of international peace and brotherhood—all this right on the premises, all mine in exchange for spending my days doing nothing, or what felt like nothing. Where would I find something better?

Indeed, I often ask myself that question.

Although my Russian and my newly acquired French are, as noted, superfluous in the job where I've ended up, the hiring process mysteriously included an eight-hour language-proficiency test, and just as mysteriously, the word "translator" figures prominently in my title. With some luck, in a few years I might transfer back to a post where foreign languages could prove useful.

In the meantime, I've decided to read Proust. Yes — *In Search of Lost Time*. In the original French. All of it. Seven volumes. On the subway. Standing up.

Here's the drill. In the morning I get to the subway platform, pull out the book, and open to the page where I left off the previous evening when the subway doors glided apart at my stop. It's a fine edition, with the thinnest of paper, the title tooled in gilt on the spine, and a slender grosgrain bookmark sewn in, also gilt. Failure to get the volume into position before the train pulls in means I may not get to do any reading that morning, as it's often too crowded to fumble in my bag for the book after I board.

Other things to do before I push my way onto the train: lay my hands on a pen in my bag and make sure the sticky note inside the book's back cover has not come unglued and fallen out. The pen and the little yellow scrap of paper are for writing down unfamiliar words. If I don't have a pen at the ready, or if the sticky note is missing or already filled with scrawls from previous commutes, I'll go back later, reread the pages, and write down the unfamiliar words I didn't capture on the first pass. Then I'll look them up during the slow moments at the office that add up to a workday, and another and another. The office with the river view is awash in battered foreign-language dictionaries that appear to have languished there for decades. If it weren't for Proust and my compulsion to look up every single unfamiliar word I come across, they would get very little use indeed.

Here are a few entries from my Proust word list: *maussade, minaudier, ondine, alambiqué, mièvre, œillet, allégresse, goûter, gazouiller, tapissier, scélératesse, entremetteuse, bristol,* and *lévrier.* Meaning, respectively: sullen, simpering, water sprite, convoluted, mawkish, carnation, jubilation, tea party, to warble, upholsterer, villainy, procuress, calling card, and greyhound.

I'm on the Seventh Avenue Express now, hurtling downtown. In one hand I hold the book, and in the other, the pen, so I cannot properly be called a straphanger. I assume a wide stance, bend my knees, and ride the train like a skateboard. In the twelve minutes or so it takes the train to barrel down the line from 96th Street to Times Square, I fight inertia's pull toward free fall into some stranger's lap, plunging instead into the bucolic village of Combray or the Paris salons and cafés where representatives of the haute bourgeoisie and the demimonde cross paths.

I read Proust almost exclusively on the subway. On weekends I rarely pick up the book; the little volume with the grosgrain marker lies untouched on my desk from Friday evening (time of unseemly rejoicing) until Monday morning (time of dread beyond reason). This runs counter to my notion of myself as someone with an almost religious reverence for literature and its greats. But there it is: my life yields up few moments that are conducive to the concentration and discipline that Proust requires. At home, I'm prey to a restlessness that is incompatible with Proust. I putter obsessively, trying to prevent the detritus of daily life—bills, dirty dishes, voice mail—from accumulating until it topples over and crushes me beneath its weight. So, month after month, I commute and read, read and commute, and now—nine months since I began—I find myself creeping up on the seven-hundred-page mark.

Every week or two I indulge in a dalliance with some other author. This sometimes takes place on the subway, but mostly off. (Often, I read these other books while sprawled on the couch.) When I read on the down low, it's always in English (no need to keep a running lookup list, with the attendant pen and Post-it note), usually the work of some contemporary author whose style is relatively terse (though compared to Proust *everything* seems terse). I can tear through a contemporary novel of two to three hundred pages in the time it takes to read twenty-five to thirty pages of Proust.

You might think that I deliberately reserve Proust for the subway because Proust and the subway are in some way uniquely compatible. Perhaps I do; perhaps they are. Reading in bursts of twelve minutes or less while standing on a subway train may not seem like the best way to absorb Proust's leisurely cadences and looping syntax, the minute perceptions captured and sliced lengthwise to reveal their delicate innards and seeds. In Proust's day, there were those who said that no serious literary work could result from writing while reclining in bed in a dressing gown. Proust paid them no mind. He wrote in bed in his dressing gown; I read on the subway. Back and forth I ride, back and forth, and slowly I advance, boring through the book like a termite through wood, at the rate of five pages each way; sometimes ten; or sometimes, during exhausting stretches of insignificant busyness, none.

Read in brief spurts, Proust's three thousand pages (well, the seven hundred I've read thus far) reveal themselves to be a series of hundreds and hundreds of linked, discursive essays two to five pages long. Here is a description of a bouquet of chrysanthemums in Madame Swann's chambers, which segues into mention of a sunset whose color is similar to the flowers', which doglegs into a discussion of how her former life as a kept woman (with a sideline in prostitution) nurtured in Odette (as she is known to her numerous intimates) a taste for a range of luxury goods delivered to her door from exclusive establishments spanning many arrondissements. Here is an examination of the difference between the face a famous writer presents at a dinner party and his interior life as laid bare in his books, and of the young narrator's astonishment at the contrast between these two aspects of the man whose work he has long admired—a contrast so marked that he thinks the party guest must in fact be some *other* writer who coincidentally bears the same name. Here is a meditation on a musical phrase that lodges in Swann's memory after repeated hearings, expanding his soul as the aroma of a rose does one's nostrils; the fragment of melody coming to signify happiness, love, moonlight, the sea, rejuvenation, a newfound interest in life, and the abandonment of a habitual tone of detachment and irony. Here is . . .

. . . Times Square. I almost missed it, engrossed in a description of the acacia trees and the public toilet on the Champs-Élysées near where Marcel and Gilberte play hide-and-seek after school. I pause midsentence, ride the human wave off the train, and come to rest on the platform. Later, when I resume reading, I will cast around in the middle of a two-page paragraph to find my place—although in a three-hundred-page stretch in which Proust places under a microscope the narrator's love for his playmate, his pain when he decides to cut himself off from the girl because she does not love him back, his brief conversations with her parents when he visits her house (at hours carefully chosen so that the girl will not be there and, hearing about his visit later, will perhaps be intrigued), and how Odette accessorizes the kimonos she wears when receiving guests, whether I resume exactly where I left off, inadvertently skip ahead, or reread half a page without realizing it right away is of almost no consequence.

I come up the stairs and cross a wide underground space on my way to board the shuttle to Grand Central, and before I see them, I hear them. The warm, ludic sounds evoke an involuntary smile, and I follow the music to the top of the stairs, around the corner, and behind a wide pillar. I stop to soak up the feeling that rolls off these musicians. They are playing a washboard, a dulcimer, a fiddle, a tambourine, cymbals, drums, a banjo, and a bass, though not all at once, as the instrument-to-player ratio is about two to one.

Dollar bills and CDs spill out of an open instrument case. The men are wearing odds and ends reminiscent of other worlds and times: a bolo tie, a bandanna, a striped railroad cap, a cowboy hat, a stocking cap pulled down low over dreadlocks. With them is a woman who wears her excess flesh like an ermine stole and passes out flyers to the sparse audience, which is constantly dispersing and replenishing itself. When she runs out of flyers, or audience, she shimmies to the music in a manner that is deeply introspective.

The flyers and the handwritten sign propped against the instrument case announce that these are the Ebony Hillbillies. The men are not young. The calm they radiate is not a natural fit with Times Square at rush hour, but, utterly at home in their music-making, they carry it off. Their attitude captivates: kindly, never rushed, each one engrossed in his own playing and simultaneously adjusting to his partners in numerous infinitesimal ways. They are doing their thing and doing it to perfection.

Soon I will hasten toward the low-cost mortgages, the cappuccino bar, the Arabic lessons, the Pilates, and the raspberries with whipped cream—I am always precisely ten minutes late, and no one in the office ever seems to notice—but for the moment I am swept up. Where do these men live? I wonder. It's always the first question a New Yorker asks. Do they ride the A train in from Far Rockaway? Maybe they've come in from Jersey City on the PATH train? Do they have day jobs? Benefits? I doubt that anyone has ever gazed admiringly at their dental insurance cards.

They play. They strum, click, scrape, and saw. One of them taps his toes, another stamps his heel, a third does something like singing but less melodious. They do not look like the kind of street musicians who interrupt their playing to bob their heads and say, *Thank you, ma'am*, to passersby dropping coins into their case. No, they are not that kind.

I stand off to the side, watching and listening for as long as I can before running to make my connection.

I head for the shuttle, which goes ceaselessly back and forth between Times Square and Grand Central. I have my pick of three trains on parallel tracks numbered 1, 3, and 4: they all go to the same place. Someone once explained to me why there's no Track 2, but I have forgotten the reason. There's a Track 2 elsewhere in the system, but it peters out before reaching Times Square. Something like that.

I clutch the little volume in one hand, preparing to open it and regain my place, midsentence. Behind me, the men—Did they grow up together somewhere in east Tennessee? Did their group coalesce in a bar in Brooklyn before Brooklyn was hip? Are they Harlem-born and -bred?—are still at it.

On the shuttle, I'll read one more page, maybe two if I recognize all the words, about Odette and the ladies who come to her Wednesday afternoons and discuss where they have their dresses made, or about a brothel where the madam always urges Marcel to try out a Jewish prostitute with messy hair—she's better educated and a better conversationalist than the others, says the madame—and Marcel always demurs: *No thank you. Maybe next time.*

I will get off the shuttle at Grand Central with the other passengers and traverse the station's cathedral-like expanse. There are easier, faster routes to work, but a day that brings with it a sense of awe, head tilted back to take in that vast space, is a day not yet entirely lost.

I will admire the pearly faced clock that anchors the center of the grand hall; go down a narrow, marble-floored passage where vendors sell grilled Hawaiian tuna, peppercorn sausage, cheeses that verge exquisitely on the foul, mangoes, Bananas Foster cupcakes (whatever *they* are), tiramisu cake, and other treats with names fancy beyond recall, wrapped in crinkly paper or packed in bright tins and dripping with snob appeal.

I will emerge from underground into the city and the shadow of the green glass building.

I cannot hear the music anymore.

Fait Accompli

2.

I WORE MY flannel nightgown with the tiny lavender flowers. Aleksandr had on his beige briefs with the blue pinstripe, he said. I filled in the rest—ruddy hair, hazel eyes, slim form. He murmured to me over thousands of kilometers of telephone wire from his home, far to the south, in Tbilisi. His voice was warm.

In 1988, no one called it phone sex. We had discovered it on our own. We were making the best of our separation.

I was sprawled on a bed in the October Revolution Hotel, gripping the receiver. Outside, a massive ship the color of lead stood at anchor in the Neva River. An enormous lamp on deck sent a beam through my window, providing practically the only illumination in all of late-night Leningrad.

"And one day, when we make love," he was saying, "it will be different from the other times, because we will make a baby." His voice turned gravelly with desire. "We'll create life. And you will become—a mother." A detailed how-to followed.

I was in the USSR working on a cultural exchange project and polishing my college Russian. I was twenty-two. Aleksandr was twenty-five, a rising star at a research institute specializing in honeybees. He inseminated the queens, artificially, using his own patented device. The bees adored him; he rarely got stung.

He had never been west of Montenegro. Inviting him to meet the folks was an undertaking. After I returned home to upstate New York, we waited eight months for the Soviet government to grant him an exit visa so he could come out for a visit. In those days, before email, cell phones, and Skype, I spent hours upon hours pressing redial, waiting for one of the four international phone lines serving his hometown to open up so that we could bellow to each other, at two dollars a minute, through a staticky roar that sounded like a volcano erupting over and over.

Years would pass before we became husband and wife. During those years of waiting, he talked frequently about the babies we would make. Before conceiving, he said, we must develop healthy habits, ingest the right minerals, avoid the wrong ones, exercise.

His health-consciousness was impressive, considering where he came from: a part of the world where liquor flows so freely that it takes real effort to become known as a serious drinker, a place where the mention of lung cancer evokes a shrug and a smoke ring. After all, what is a demise at home, at your own pace, a death you choose yourself, compared to the midnight knock at the door, disappearance, interrogation, the gulag with its attendant frostbite, starvation, execution, all still part of recent memory? With that as the alternative, dying at home is a pleasure, a luxury, an assertion of free will.

Aleksandr was a nonsmoker; that alone made him remarkable in his world. He drank in moderation. By putting fishing line to novel use, he had independently discovered dental floss, a commodity unheard of in the Soviet Union.

And so, before we could become parents, we must be "ready." Whatever that meant. But that was fine. My twenties and thirties stretched ahead. So far ahead that I could not see where they might lead. I listened to Aleksandr's voice and I followed.

———————

Three years after that telephone conversation, three years marked by extended visits and protracted separations, we were married near his parents' home in Georgia. The next morning, the bedroom door flew open. We threw on some clothes.

In bustled Aleksandr's chubby maiden aunt, Tamara, who lived in the apartment downstairs, pulling a little girl by the hand. The child was her namesake, and she went by the nickname Tamrico. She was one of the cousins, a ringleted five-year-old who often wore an enormous pink bow. We called her Tamrico the Terrible. During the wedding photos the day before, she had smashed her tiny fist through the lens of the only camera the family owned.

Behind the two Tamaras, other family members hovered.

"There's something little Tamrico wants to know," said Tamara the Elder, laughing. We rubbed our eyes and blinked.

"Come on," she said to the little girl. "What did you just say downstairs? Remember? Say it again."

Tamrico took a breath. She recited: "Now that you're married, when will you have a baby?"

A few years later, when Aleksandr and I were living in Philadelphia, his mother Nadezhda flew over for a visit. She set her suitcase down by the door, let her shearling coat slip off her shoulders onto the nearest chair, and set out on a circuit of the apartment.

"I've found the perfect place for the crib," she said when she was done. The look on her exotic, youthful features was dreamy, yet practical.

Crib?

"Where?"

"By your side of the bed," she said to me. "So when the baby cries at night, you'll be right there. And it's far from the window, away from drafts."

Similar comments followed in a steady stream. After a few days, Aleksandr and I shut ourselves in the bedroom to confer.

"We'll say it's my fault we don't have a child yet," he declared suddenly. "You want a baby, but I'm not ready."

He had been born precisely ten months after his parents' wedding day, so we were way overdue. I appreciated his willingness to take the heat.

I cannot pinpoint the moment when this story became the truth.

———————

Around us, people started having children. People younger than we were. People with less money. We fished and skied. These were Aleksandr's favorite pastimes. In bad weather, we went to the mall and browsed for goggles and lures.

"When will we have a child?" I asked at the Jersey shore, the waves lapping at our ankles.

"We aren't ready," he said, casting his line into the surf.

"When will we have a child?" I asked on the chairlift at Sugarloaf.

"We aren't ready," he said, banging a pole against his binding. Chunks of snow floated down onto the trail.

Those who can't conceive go to fertility specialists. What specialist could help here? I cursed birth control in all its forms; the more reliable it was, the more I resented it. Once on the pill, I was not free to go off it of my own accord, despite some advice from Nadezhda that came in a phone call one day when Aleksandr was out.

"Present him with a fait accompli!" she suggested. Her mischievous laughter echoed from halfway around the world.

———————

In the sixth year of our marriage, we went to a Caribbean island. Seated under a thatched awning, we stared at the sea. We removed the miniature umbrellas from our drinks and shook the sweet drops into our glasses. I said something about a baby.

"Please," he said, "don't spoil my vacation."

A week after we got home, I uttered the B-word again. Aleksandr said, "I had a long day at work. I'm tired."

When I mentioned the dreaded word in the kitchen, he drifted into the living room.

His list of objections grew and grew. Pregnancy would make me fat. If we had a baby, we would stop having sex. We couldn't afford a child. We couldn't cope without extended family nearby.

"What if I, uh, get pregnant by accident?"

"You'll get an abortion," he answered promptly. "Our baby must be planned."

Planned. What did that mean? At the supermarket, women with fractious toddlers and wailing infants counted out the food stamps. They could have children. Why couldn't I?

I dreamed I was pregnant. Men in white lab coats subdued me. I was lashed to a table.

Gleaming implements were raised high above my belly.

"I've been thinking," he said in that warm voice of his. "I'm almost ready."

Someone had warned me that he might react this way.

"Ready," I repeated dully. "Ready for what?"

I knew what his answer would be, and I knew already that it meant nothing. But even now, at this late stage, at this stage that was too late for anything at all, I still thought I wanted to hear him say it.

"To have that baby." He paused. "I hope it's a girl with big black eyes and curly hair. Like you."

"When?"

"Maybe in a year. Maybe two years. Not quite yet."

I was barely listening.

A few times during the subsequent, solitary years, I found myself dining across from men in their late forties who seemed unnervingly attached to me on the basis of a very brief acquaintance indeed. I was in my early thirties. Then my middle thirties. I was their last hope. I could bear their children, they thought. Those men would have been disappointed. I would be disappointed.

———————

I might never have written any of this down, except for what happened as forty loomed. A jog of ten blocks left me gasping for breath. Climbing the stairs made my heart race. How had I gotten so out of shape while exercising regularly? After each incident, my breathing returned to normal, and I forgot that anything out of the ordinary had occurred.

There came a morning when I felt a stabbing in my chest. And then I was prone in the emergency room.

The doctor studied the X-rays.

"Your lung has collapsed," she said.

Tristan, my boyfriend of one year, was at my bedside. He had forgotten to take off his black lambswool hat with the silky flaps like a puppy's ears.

"Your husband will have to step outside while we insert the shunt," said a nurse.

"We'll ask your husband to hold your clothes," said another.

I liked the sound of it.

When the nurses stepped away to get supplies, I seized the fringes of his red and green plaid scarf and pulled him down toward me.

"Will you marry me?" I croaked.

He looked as if he had been startled out of a reverie, a look he often had.

"Of course," he said, as if it had been settled long ago.

Home from the hospital, I darted into the bathroom, leaned over, and watched as the contents of my stomach slid into the toilet. We set a wedding date. I went off the pill.

One evening when I was strong again, he swung a leg over

mine and said with a grin, "So, are we going to make a baby tonight?"

We tried. No baby. We tried. Oh, baby, how we tried.

Five months later, my lung collapsed again.

A biopsy was taken, and that was when I learned about the rare, incurable pulmonary condition with the eleven-syllable name. I'd never heard of it. No one I knew had ever heard of it.

Around the time Tristan and I got married, three months after the diagnosis, a leading specialist told me somberly, "In your condition, pregnancy would be very dangerous indeed." There were further consultations, a second opinion, a third. Everyone agreed.

More years have passed. I'm standing in a schoolyard, off to the side, by the fence, my eyes glued to a blue baseball cap about three and a half feet above the ground. Fixing my gaze on the cap is the best way to keep track of the small person who is my flesh and blood as he tears around the yard with the other first-graders.

This little boy was hard won. He arrived after two miscarriages and tens of thousands of dollars in fertility treatments.

He is my sister's boy. My sister has just had surgery for bunions, and for several weeks she'll barely be able to take a step. And so I walk my nephew to school while his mother sits on the sofa, her foot immobilized in a cast. Medical woes have their upside, if they are someone else's and not too grave.

Meanwhile, my lungs are now functioning at less than fifty per cent of normal capacity and declining still.

Most of the parents bring their children to school a few minutes early and stand watching them play, until the impossibly young teachers come out and lead their charges inside to start the day.

A man in his early forties stands not far from me, near the fence. He's wearing a maroon baseball jacket, number forty-four.

Nearby is a little boy wearing number twenty-two. The man glances over at me. He tries to catch my eye. He takes a step toward me.

A pregnant silence takes shape. I let it grow and grow. My wedding ring is concealed inside my glove.

Finally, jerking his head toward the bobbing mass of children, he asks, "Whose mom are you?"

The Bagels in the Snowflake

2.

OUTSIDE, THERE WERE LOTS. Block after block. Deserted. Some had been parking lots and were now home to abandoned wrecks, as if people had parked, shoved their car keys into a pocket, and wandered off. Then years had passed, years of entropy and rust, and after a while there was no longer any reason to park here because once you got out of your car there was no place to go.

There were other lots with no cars. These were not parking lots. They were marked by heaps of rubble that had once been businesses or homes.

Outside, there was also a burnt-out supermarket, its windows laid out in jagged jigsaw puzzles on the sidewalk before it. Outside, there were rows of brick boxes: public housing.

Inside, there were bagels: poppy seed, sesame, garlic, salt, plain. No blueberry, no whole wheat, nothing with raisins. This was in the seventies, before the secularization of the bagel. There were onion-flecked bialy rolls, named in honor of the Polish town of Bialystok, once home to large numbers of Jews who had loved their town devotedly, according to the histories, until they were killed there, every last one, except those few who hid under the bodies in the mass graves, feigned death, and burrowed their way out after the executioners went home for dinner. There was pumpernickel, its musky fragrance and chocolaty color hinting richly at the molasses within. Caraway seeds riding atop loaves of rye bread like docile passengers on a train. Challah speckled with poppy seeds, awaiting its dusting of Friday-evening prayer.

Outside, all was gray. The sky. The concrete ground. Gray. Inside, all was golden and fragrant.

The Snowflake Bakery was once at the heart of a Jewish neighborhood in my hometown of Syracuse, New York. Then the neighborhood's residents, still nomadic (it takes more than a generation or two of settled life to forget millennia of wandering), migrated to the suburbs.

For a time, the bakery remained, a small oasis of bustle and warmth anchoring concentric circles of urban desolation. The glass cases in the unadorned front room were heaped with bread and cake. The shelves lining the walls held stacks of folded cardboard, with slots and flaps designed for assembly into elegant white and blue boxes.

Most fascinating for a child were the mysterious metal bulbs suspended from the ceiling over the counter. A worker would give a quick tug on the end of a piece of twine (also white and blue, to match the boxes) sticking out at the bottom of the bulb, foot after foot of string would be disgorged, and the worker would flip the box rapidly over and over, over and over, bundling the purchases deftly and securely.

We went to the Snowflake often and left bearing shiny white bags and boxes with patterns of large, symmetrical navy-blue snowflakes on them. The bags ballooned with aromas. In addition to bread, the Snowflake had all kinds of sweets: rugelach, babke, and wedding cake, to name just a few. For years and years, a dusty, superannuated plastic bride and groom stood atop a sample wedding cake on a high shelf, turning slowly from white to gray (the cake as well as the couple) in a touching display of constancy.

The nameless yellow cookies, oblong, with ridges, tipped with colored sprinkles, and filled with jam were, for me, the most important merchandise on offer there. Then and especially later, after I had traveled a bit, I knew in my heart that these yellow cookies and all others like them belonged to me, all of them, wherever in the world they might be. I learned this because every time we went into the bakery, someone would lean across the counter, tell my mother that I was adorable, and reach down to hand me one of them in a twist of wax paper. (I never noticed if it was the same person each time; I was too small to get a good look over the counter, and adults did not interest me much.) The cookie was an offering laid at the altar of childhood. I received it graciously. I ate it fast.

The bakery was my sole passageway to a world whose existence I barely suspected and to which I was, nonetheless, intimately linked; the world of my fathers. The world of my fathers, before belief and rituals extending back millennia were let go like balloons sailing off into the sky. In leaving it all behind, my grandparents (for that was when it mostly happened, two generations before me) were breaking free to join the big world. In doing so, they were in step with their times; times of doubt, turmoil, and revolution.

But now, all that remained to us was the bread. I had never stepped inside a synagogue, but I imagined that a Jewish holy place would look something like the Snowflake; it was the only Jewish place I knew. Even now, when I read in some Yiddish novel that someone has gone to a synagogue, I imagine the character davening in the Snowflake, surrounded by fragrant loaves like well-wishing congregants. Never mind that the Snowflake had nothing in common with any shul I have since read about or visited, not one with a soaring ceiling, a women's gallery, and an ornate Torah stand; nor a dim, cramped prayer house, a *shtibele*, for humble folk, tailors, or milliners; nor an angular structure in the suburbs, a way station on the route to assimilation.

What has bread to do with prayer, or a bakery with a shul? I am still not sure, but I made the connections that I needed to make. I wanted to stay inside the bakery. I wanted to live there. When we came outside, arms full of bread, I felt the chill of exile.

Our Judaism may have been submerged, diluted, but our family was different from those among whom we lived. There were signs that could not be ignored. We were swarthier than most of our neighbors. And we didn't celebrate Christmas. Why no Christmas? When I learned to speak and to ask questions, this was explained to me anew each year, in tones of increasing exasperation, until I was about ten and could finally retain the answer:

"Because we are Jews, and Christmas is a Christian holiday!"

I had a hard time grasping that Christmas was off-limits, because we didn't celebrate anything else, except Thanksgiving. Most people I knew who didn't celebrate Christmas celebrated other things that people who celebrated Christmas didn't celebrate.

Another sign of our difference: other people I knew bought sliced white bread at the supermarket in plastic bags with pictures of balloons and a twist tie, while we made a special trip to the Snowflake. We ate brown loaves, round loaves, loaves with seeds, braided loaves. When I brought sandwiches on challah to school, the boys taunted me. "Yellow bread!" they yelled. Apparently this was a term of opprobrium. No one had ever seen anything like it.

Bread was the biggest difference that I could see between us and others. But bread, I sensed, was a surface manifestation of something deeper, a difference that remained impossible to grasp.

———————

"We aren't really Jewish, you know. We just like to eat Jewish bread." My sister said this to me one day when she was twelve and I was six.

All my life I'd been hearing that we were Jewish, although what that might mean had never been explained. If I'd been sent to a mainline Protestant Sunday school, I would have known more about the history of the Jews than I learned as a secular Jewish child. I would not learn who Moses was, what the Exodus was, until long after I graduated from an Ivy League university and decided that it was time to engage in some independent study.

But I was nonetheless shocked to hear at age six that we weren't really Jewish. Had I been lied to all my life? How could this thing, which I imagined to be far deeper than bread, be only about bread? If my sister was right, I had lost something important before I even knew what it was.

Was she playing a trick, as older siblings do? Telling me something outrageous and incredible to sow panic and shore up her own authority? I doubt even she could answer now; this happened some four decades ago, if indeed I am not imagining it. But I think that she too believed what she told me: *It's all about the bread.* She too was struggling to figure things out.

We had pumpernickel, rye, bagels, and challah, yet there was no Friday night ritual in our house involving challah — it was merely one of the building blocks of peanut butter and jelly sandwiches. Pumpernickel, rye, bagels, and challah were what we had. Hamantaschen, never. Matzoh, never. These were too closely tied to holidays that we did not mark.

Apart from bread, what were the other signs that we were Jewish? I wondered. Probably my sister wondered too.

I went to my brother first; he was the oldest and he had taught me to read. His bedroom was at the top of the house. He emerged from the crawl space behind his closet, smelling of something smoky and sweet. I heard voices coming from the crawl space. On the turntable Deep Purple was singing.

"Aren't we Jewish?" I asked, looking way up to search his face for an answer.

He looked distracted. With a glance toward the secret place behind the closet where his friends waited, he said kindly, "Go ask Mom."

My mother was hanging up laundry. "Of course we're Jewish," she said briskly, between clothespins. "What makes you think otherwise?"

I mumbled something and engulfed myself between two halves of a queen-sized sheet draped on the line. When I emerged from the damp folds, I felt the connection once more.

The Snowflake was holy again; it was once again the link whereby everything would someday come clear, though I did not then know how. Years later, I would imagine a door in the back, behind the counter, leading to an enchanted field—not a wreck-strewn parking lot—where a small goat, perfectly white but for a six-pointed black star on its forehead, sprawled gracefully as in some Yiddish ballad, effortlessly representing purity and innocence. Next to the goat, a man with a long beard might be readying himself and the little beast for the journey to Jerusalem. He would coax the goat to its feet, wait for it to stop wobbling on its tiny hooves, and gently place a rope around its neck, leading it far, far away, toward sunrise.

But the bakery was failing. It was slowly going the way of the burnt-out supermarket. When I was nine, it cut back to three days a week. A year later, it moved to a warehouse with no storefront and became a wholesale supplier to restaurants and remote suburban grocery stores. If the proprietor came to the phone, and if he was in a good mood, he might offer a loyal customer a few loaves left over from a large commercial order, sometimes giving them away for free with a magnanimous wave of the hand when we arrived to pick them up and sometimes demanding an exorbitant price he had clearly thought up on the spot. Whatever he asked, we paid it. He was doing us a favor.

But such unpredictable arrangements could not be relied on to provide bread for a family of five on a regular basis. My parents pondered the matter of bread. As a stopgap, we got the plastic bags from the grocery, the ones with the pictures of balloons and the twist tie. Briefly, we seemed like everyone else. (I never found a secret door; no little white goat stepped along the path. The snowflake melted and the sacred bakery disappeared, leaving only a trail of crumbs leading I know not where.)

Then a solution was found, and the Wonder Bread era drew to a close. We began patronizing an Italian bakery just under the highway that led out of town to the airport. It sold long, thick loaves and round, flat ones, both baked from the same dough. That was all. The flat loaves were designed to be ripped apart, not sliced, along indentations that were baked in.

This bakery was a fearsome, primitive place; a dim, flour-coated hole directly in the path of the exhaust fumes pouring off the overpass. Workers wearing immense black mitts flung open the cast-iron doors of the stone ovens, using massive wooden paddles to maneuver the loaves in and out. The paddles appeared designed for use by giants to spank smaller giants who had misbehaved. The ovens were large enough to roast a medium-sized animal on a spit.

The bakery belonged to a family of immigrants who had clearly come from someplace unspeakably abject. The grown daughters, in thrall to their evil-tempered father, looked oppressed and bitter in their white aprons streaked with soot.

But if you arrived at the right moment, the bread, too hot to touch, was just coming out of the oven on its paddles, and we would buy out the whole place, or nearly, getting so many loaves that we had to press hard on the trunk of the car to make it close.

On the ride home, we were allowed to rip up one loaf and eat it. We moaned and sucked our burnt fingers as wisps of vapor released from the very center of the bread floated around inside the car.

Haunting Synagogues

2.

Each stone a book; parchment every wall.
Pages turn, secretly open in the night.
—Moyshe Kulbak, "Vilne"
(translated from Yiddish by Nathan Halper)

STROLLING ALONG in the West Seventies near Riverside Park recently, I passed the building where Aleksandr and I lived awhile before we were married. This was some twenty-one years ago.

The mover brought our things up. We didn't have much; one mover was more than enough. He set down his load.

"Maybe you won't be here too long," he said, kindly.

It was a day or two before I fully grasped the situation: the place we'd moved into—the tarnished sign in front said Imperial Court, in cursive, silver-colored letters—was something less than an apartment building. (Aleksandr, a recent arrival from a distant land, could not have been expected to be alert to the cues—that was my job.) Old women shuffled in the hallways, their fat feet packaged in brown paper secured with twine. Rent was due weekly, cash only. When I dialed my parents to tell them that we had settled in and everything was fine, I found that long-distance service was blocked, and no amount of importuning the clerk downstairs would get it connected.

Local calls were thirty-five cents. You could not run a tab. You hung up the phone and you went downstairs with your quarter and your dime or two nickels, if you were relatively solvent, or else your fistful of pennies collected from the backs of drawers and under the upholstery. If you came up short and thought of biding your time upstairs until you had to pass the front desk the next day on your way to work (if you had a job), you would get a call from the front desk within minutes, even if it was three in the morning, reminding you that you had incurred a debt that must be wiped out *now*.

A moaning came across the air shaft. Usually on Sunday afternoons. It would crescendo, peak, cease, begin again. And again. And, sometimes, again.

On a rainy Sunday in May, the climaxes came and came, one and then another, fast, five, six, seven.

From a nearby room, a man called out wearily, "Okay, enough!"

Silence settled over the air shaft.

We wondered about every woman we passed in the hallways, those who had their feet bundled in brown paper, and those few who did not: is she the One?

Next door was a tiny redbrick building, one story tall, squeezed between Imperial Court on one side, and on the other, a regular apartment building with a uniformed doorman and plantings in large earthenware pots flanking the entrance. I gave the tiny building in the middle barely a glance when I went by. I was past it in two strides: what was to see?

On certain nights that seemed somehow different from all others, people in elegant, dark clothes clustered before it. They appeared well acquainted with one another. Perhaps even related. The women's hair, what I could glimpse of it beneath hats and scarves, looked glossy and stiff.

I would hasten home from work as the weekend began, hoping that I could get by the little building before the people collected. I did not want to be seen in my office clothes, heading into an ordinary evening of rice and beans eaten from one plate with two forks, side by side on the floor or the futon, itself on the floor, followed by a movie or a stroll. I left the office at the same time each day, but I didn't always make it home early enough to avoid the crowd: the meeting time in front of the little building varied over the course of the year according to some factor I could not, at the time, divine.

The clues multiplied. I could no longer ignore what sort of place this was. Those little crowds made me uneasy. I should be standing with those people, I felt obscurely, and I should be dressed up like them. I should go with them inside the tiny building at the appointed hour, and I should be familiar with whatever it was that went on within its recesses.

Despite my sense that there was some action I ought to take, something that, owing to the circumstances of my birth, it behooved me to know and to do, during the fourteen months we lived next door to that building, I never once went inside and never once exchanged a word with any of the people there.

And then we left Imperial Court—abruptly—after a cockroach fell out of the book I was reading, landed on its back on my pillow, then righted itself and traversed the bed with a purposeful gait, and finally passed through a hole near the foot of the mattress, entering another dimension. I learned much, much later that the place next door was presided over by one Rabbi Shlomo Carlebach, one of the most famous rabbis in the world and the scion of a distinguished Hasidic dynasty going back centuries.

Those people who stood on the sidewalk every week as the sun sank across the Hudson River were an enigma to me. As far as I knew, barely anyone practiced Judaism any more, except a tiny number of devotees who probably traveled by horse-drawn buggy and did without electricity.

The Jews I knew were university professors, mostly, plus a few doctors and lawyers. They did not believe, did not practice, did not pray. The walls of their homes were lined with books of all kinds, secular ones. Their politics ran the gamut from liberal to left wing. And a gamut it was: market socialist, Labor Zionist, anarchist, fellow traveler, Maoist, Trotskyist, Stalinist. Some of the older men had served in the Abraham Lincoln Brigade; their wives had chaired committees at the Women's International League for Peace and Freedom.

To the extent that they honored the faith of their ancestors, they did so by telling jokes about old ladies with Yiddish accents. Old ladies who themselves might or might not be religiously observant. These Jews I knew sometimes ate lox and bagels or bialy rolls or rye bread with caraway seeds. They knew some Yiddish words. They uttered them occasionally, and when they did so, listeners would chuckle knowingly, wryly, as if to say: *I have heard words in this language before, and, though dead, it is very lovable.*

This was the sum total of my knowledge about the Jews. Of whom I was one.

––––––––––

But anyone who concludes that I come from people who did not go to synagogues would be mistaken.

My father's father, for example: at age seven, he made up his mind to fast on the Day of Atonement, in the face of parental opposition and without regard for the fact that young children, like the elderly, the sick and the pregnant, are not expected to go hungry on Yom Kippur. At ten in the morning on that holiest day of the year, seated on a hard pew in Brooklyn, he fainted and slid to the floor.

My father loved telling that story. (He fainted! From hunger! On Yom Kippur! At ten in the morning! Roars of laughter invariably followed.) But if that earnest little boy who would become my grandfather hadn't collapsed in the synagogue, and if his collapse had not become family legend, I would not have learned until much, much later that any member of my family had ever stepped inside a shul.

I was in my thirties when I found out that my maternal grandfather had also been in one of those institutions, or more than one, apparently on a somewhat regular basis.

We were emptying out my Aunt Esther's apartment in Chicago at the end of her life. Her closets were stuffed with decades' worth of accumulated dresses and shoes. Dozens of tubes of lipstick crammed the bathroom shelves. Perfumes too, with names like *Obsession*, *Poison*, *Opium*, and *Surrender*. For years I had seen the graceful little flasks, some still nearly full, others empty, their contents used up or evaporated.

And the blue velvet pouch with the Hebrew letters embroidered on it was there, in the bedroom, in a tattered wicker basket, at the exact center of a heap of ragged bath towels I was folding and stacking for the Salvation Army. Inside the pouch was a silky blue-and-white strip of cloth edged on two sides with fringe. I had never held one of these in my hands before. The gold embroidered characters were sheerest gibberish to me.

I have since learned to decipher them: they spell out the word *tallis*, meaning prayer shawl. The pouch and its contents now occupy a spot on the shelf over my desk. No one else wanted them; I asked everyone who might conceivably lay a claim. I took them from the laundry basket that day and brought them home. I often look at the letters and take pleasure in sounding them out: *tallis*.

In Aunt Esther's bedroom that day, I spread the shimmering fabric across my hands and turned to my mother. She was going through the drawers of the vanity table next to the double bed where for many, many years, my aunt had slept alone, and sometimes not.

"Who did this belong to?" I asked, astonished. It was the only Jewish ritual object I had ever come across in our family, and the only Jewish ritual object I had ever seen up close.

"Oh," said my mother, peering at the cloth draped over my hands. "That must have belonged to my father."

She started to turn back to the mirror. I sat very still.

Slowly, she faced me again.

"He used to go to the synagogue sometimes," she said. "When he was a young man. Back in Lithuania, and later on, in Chicago. To keep his father company."

————————

And now I remember that I once stepped into a synagogue back home in Syracuse. Accompanied by my parents. I was in college: it was 1984, and *Shoah* had just been released. It was screened in the sanctuary of a place called Beth Israel on a street that led out of town toward the mall that was home to the local JC Penney.

The screen must have been set up in front of the ark. I say this because now I know what an ark is and that every synagogue has one, and I did not see one in that synagogue. So that ornamental repository that holds the Torah scrolls must have been hidden behind the screen on which images of overgrown fields, abandoned buildings, and talking heads were projected. Claude Landzmann, the director of *Shoah*, famously chose not to use period photographs or footage, conjuring the horror with nothing more than the words and memories of survivors, perpetrators, and bystanders. No gas chambers, emaciated prisoners, or corpses stacked like cordwood were shown on the screen in the synagogue: no ark or Torah scroll was visible. I did not think to ask: What is this place for? What do Jews do when they gather here, apart from watching nine-hour documentaries on the systematic near obliteration of their—our—people?

————————

And now all the synagogues are rushing toward me, bearing down, then passing by and receding, like cars on the highway:

synagogues from various years, synagogues I walked past, synagogues I lived near, synagogues I mostly did not enter. Like an unlucky hitchhiker, I watch them go by.

One of them was of Moorish design. Long ago it had been green, but the paint was coming off in long strips. Down the street from the dilapidated hostel in Leningrad where I stayed as an exchange student during my last summer in college, it was the only synagogue in the entire city. I could easily have gone inside; it was very far from home. I could have told myself, as I went in, that I was making a tourist visit.

But there was a padlock on the massive iron door. It was always there. Day after day I went to check on that padlock: Maybe it had disappeared overnight? Sometimes small knots of people gathered outside, talking in low voices and glancing up at the turrets from time to time. I asked who held the key. I asked seven times, once for each week of my stay. No one knew. Or maybe someone knew and didn't say. Sometimes I placed one eye at the gap between the double doors and tried, tried to see inside. All was dark. Once, I thought I heard voices.

After I lived next door to the tiny building in New York City and even longer after my sojourn near the padlocked Moorish fantasy, many years passed during which the word "synagogue" did not enter my mind. Then one Saturday morning I found myself aimlessly driving around the Philadelphia neighborhood where I had been living for several years. It was as if I had awakened behind the wheel that morning after a long sleep. I was in my early thirties.

I say I was driving aimlessly, but in fact I did have a purpose, which was to avoid going home, where Aleksandr, my husband now, would soon wake up and no doubt wonder why I was not in bed beside him or somewhere nearby. Every time I drove past the house, I felt something forcefully pushing me away. And so I circled the blocks near where we lived, driving past the rambling stone houses with their old-fashioned luxuriant gardens.

I pulled up in front of a Presbyterian church.

The week before, I had heard someone at the food co-op telling her companion that a renegade New Age Jewish congregation met there in the basement on Saturday mornings. Originally, I heard her say, it had been part of a more established group called B'nai Or, meaning Brothers of Light. I sidled closer with my basket and picked up heirloom tomatoes, one by one, checking for soft spots. Then some of the members had broken away, led by a former Hasid and Vietnam vet who, said the woman, rode a motorcycle and carried a worn copy of *The Dharma Bums* in the pocket of his bomber jacket. The new group called itself P'nai Or, or Path of Light, changing one letter to eliminate the word "Brothers," so the women wouldn't feel excluded. Path of Light had no place to go, so the church offered them the use of a basement room for those few hours a week. I put three tomatoes in my basket and moved off toward the organic peanut butter.

Now I ventured inside the church. Singing came up the stairs; something was in full swing. There were people in white robes and colored robes and rainbowy, beaded kippahs, a word I didn't know yet, and people in ordinary clothes. I pulled a battered prayer book off the shelf by the door. I saw others holding similar books open before them, turning a page occasionally, more or less in unison. I sat down at the back next to a table holding stacks of fliers announcing an exercise class: Form Hebrew letters with your body!

No one seemed to see me, and I hoped that I was indeed invisible. What page were they on? I could not tell. I could not ask. I may even have been holding the prayer book upside down.

The song ended. A few people finished a beat late. A young man who seemed at least as much in charge as anyone asked a tanned, curly-haired couple to come forward. Holding hands and beaming, they did so. They would soon be going under the hup-pah, the young man said. I understood what that meant. There was cheering. People called out blessings—I think that's what they were.

They're not so young, I thought. *It could well be a second marriage for one or both of them. It is possible to begin again.* But I could not imagine how or when I might ever get to where this couple was, or with whom, or what inhospitable expanses I would have to traverse to reach that place where lilies bloom and the vines are heavy with grapes, and doves perch amidst pomegranates and figs, and goats and deer prance alongside mountain streams.

The praying and singing commenced again. I opened the book at random and stared at the page. Next to me a woman moved her lips. She glanced over at me and at the book in my hands, then held her own closer to me to indicate what page these ecstatic mystics had reached. I didn't know it then, but this is a common form of wordless assistance between strangers in synagogues the world over. Lots of people must get lost each week in the thickets of the Hebrew liturgy for this gesture to be so widespread.

When I thought no one was looking, I fled, replacing the book on the shelf on my way out. I had been there for about twenty minutes of a two-hour service.

I think of that couple still. They would be celebrating their fourteenth anniversary about now.

———

I've been inside quite a few synagogues since then. I've joined some, in places where I've lived. I've paid dues. I've murmured the Amidah and been among the last to sit down. I've recited the Sh'ma and listened as others say Kaddish. I've nailed mezuzahs to doorframes and lit Friday night candles.

After I left the sleeping Aleksandr, I began rapidly acquiring and reading Jewish books: the Torah, a gift from my uncle by marriage, who was a gentile; a siddur, given to me by a rabbi who had some extras lying around; the Haggadah, found on a shelf in the bathroom on the top floor of my parents' house. Also Saul Bellow, Bernard Malamud, Philip Roth, Joseph Roth, Henry Roth, Anzia Yezierska, Michael Gold, Aaron Appelfeld, Primo Levi, Cynthia Ozick, Amos Oz, Chaim Grade, Katya Molodowsky, Itzik Manger, Herman Wouk, Abraham Cahan—I list them here pell-mell, as I read them—Grace Paley, Sholem Aleichem, Isaac Babel, Isaac Bashevis Singer.

I've read so many books by and about Jews that if such books were bricks, the ones I've read would be sufficient to build a synagogue. A very small synagogue: one story. I've taught myself more about the history and culture of the Jews than many lifelong, faithful synagogue attendees will ever know. As they have something that I will never have—they are at home in a Jewish house of prayer, they are at home in the house of Judaism.

———————

I'm living in New York City again now, very close to where I lived twenty-one years ago, in a neighborhood with a great diversity of synagogues, and of Jews. A synagogue membership costs hundreds of dollars each year. Like many Jews, I cross the threshold just twice annually, which many see as a dropping-off in observance and a sign of assimilation, but which in my case marks a decisive and unprecedented return to my origins. But still, it is very expensive to join a synagogue, and when I was a member, I had little to show for it—the benefits are intangible.

So I quit. Just didn't renew. The synagogue habit never truly took hold. You can go to an exercise class and stretch and stretch your muscles to try and go down into a split, but if you start late in life, your goal will probably remain forever out of reach, despite your most earnest efforts.

Speaking of which, as I was leaving the gym in my sweaty exercise clothes the other day, I saw a Saturday couple walking past outside, both of them resplendent in their Shabbes millinery, upstanding. I think they were pushing a baby carriage. Or perhaps what I saw was the shadowy outline of the baby carriage to come.

When I see religious Jews in my neighborhood, I think of Jewish Warsaw in the early twentieth century, as Isaac Bashevis Singer portrayed it: wildly diverse, with secular Jews and revolutionaries living cheek-by-jowl with the *frum* (observant), sometimes in the same family. Bashevis comes to mind at such moments because I want to believe that the Jewish Upper West Side of Manhattan is the successor to that vanished, once-vibrant world, that the community holds a place for me.

Still, I did not exit the gym right away. I stood behind the glass doors and waited for the behatted, upstanding couple to pass by, then stole out behind them, unobserved.

The Book of
Disaster

2.

Yiddish is the light that twinkles in the window.
—Moyshe Kulbak, "Vilne"

PART I

Everything began in Lithuania, of course. But where to begin in
Lithuania?

I could start with my grandfather, who was born there in 1888
and left for the West when he was about seventeen. His story colors everything I'll ever say about the place, it's true, but by leaving
for America when he did, he wrote himself out of this chapter,
and I thank him for it.

I could begin with the Germans, whose Final Solution was
very nearly realized in Lithuania, with 90 percent of the Jews
there killed by war's end.

Warmer, a little warmer.

I could begin with my own journey there, in 2007.

It was then that I met Faina.

———

I arrived, and then I procrastinated. I was finding my way around,
and the Yiddish classes at the university were just getting under
way, and as the course brochure promised, they were intense.

Hours of classes every morning; in the afternoons, lectures on
history delivered by some of the lucky few who'd come through it

alive; hours of grammar every night and of reading: poems, stories, novel excerpts—the pearls of Yiddish belles lettres. I could no longer call myself a novice by any stretch; back in New York, I had taken classes upon classes, the equivalent of three years of college Yiddish. Yet with Yiddish written right to left using the *alef beys*, as the Hebrew letters are called, the alphabet fatigue was still severe. After every sentence, I stopped to rest. Cracking Cyrillic had never been like this.

I did phone the Jewish Museum, finally. Somebody named Jessica had given me the number. She'd hung out with members of the museum staff in the late nineties during her stint in the Peace Corps. On weekends, she told me, she used to crisscross the country by bus, photographing the old synagogues.

While the phone rang at the museum, I thought of her.

When the Soviets annexed Lithuania in the 1940s, she'd told me, two synagogues were left operating in the whole country, while countless others (more than a hundred in the capital alone) were shuttered or converted into warehouses, sports clubs, or stables. But they were still recognizable: Hebrew letters carved in the stone, arched windows, often boarded up, and inside, if you lifted your gaze, you'd see the gallery upstairs where, in the old days, the women used to pray.

After that, there were the secret synagogues. A high wall would go up around a house, providing cover for Shabbes, the wedding canopy, and all the rest. The sacred books in these places had their own false covers: *The Talmud* might be disguised as *The Collected Works of Lenin*.

Someone picked up.

"Good afternoon," I said in Russian. Russian has become a minority language in post-Soviet Lithuania, one that many people will speak only under duress, but it was the best I could do.

"May I please speak to Elvina?"

"She's in the hospital. She had an accident."

I glanced down at my slip of paper.

"Is Sonya there?"

"Sonya got married and moved to Spain," she said, adding a grammatical fillip that made the phrase "got married" function like a Russian verb of motion (a category usually limited to forms of "walk," "drive," "ride," and "fly"), transporting Sonya to the land of castles and castanets on a magic carpet woven out of language.

Those were all the names I had, so I ended up explaining that I was in Vilnius for a month (no need to say why; every Jew in town knew about the intensive Yiddish course that brought an influx of foreigners each summer), and that Jessica from DC had asked me to call, and it turned out that Faina had known Jessica too, and then we discovered that we were going to the same concert that evening, sponsored by the Yiddish Department.

I'm in my seventies, said Faina. Nondescript and extremely thin. I'll wear a silk scarf. Bright red.

We found each other right away.

The concert? I don't remember much. It was probably your typical twenty-first-century Yiddish fare: a skinny young blond, struggling to belt out the songs and inject some *neshome* (that's Hebrew for "soul," and it's made its way into Yiddish too, which is how I know the word at all), the way people imagine they were sung back in the day, when the Yiddish world was teetering but had not yet gone smash. Her voice was low, warm, with a hint of gravel, and she held her arms out from her sides as if she weighed a glorious two hundred and fifty pounds instead of a scrawny one-o-five. If you've been to a few of these things, you'll know what I mean.

It was a fine northern summer evening, the dark twilight coiling itself around the sky's edges and spreading slowly inward, the light never fully retreating before beginning to reappear. The temperature was perfect, like wading into a warm lake. For hours, we walked the empty streets, talking in bursts that punctuated the stillness around us. Despite her slight build and her age, Faina had an uncanny strength. She pulled me forward through the silent city.

The night was at its darkest when we came to a row of mulberry trees. As a child in upstate New York, I had stolen fruit off a tree just like these: the thin branches come straight down like bead curtains, forming a small room, completely enclosed. Berries glowed black and white in the faint light of the streetlamps and popped under our shoes.

The ground was dirt, packed hard. No grass. The end of Communism has changed nothing in this respect. I think that once there must have been grass, but it was trampled to death and never reseeded. Why? Would that be so difficult?

Faina pulled out a key on a string around her neck, and we found ourselves in a cramped living room with a china cabinet, a fake Oriental hanging on the wall, and matched sets of Chekhov, Pushkin, and the other guys in a case with a glass front. The carpet was above a sofa that no doubt folded out into a bed. I'd seen so many places like this one across the former USSR; even if I'd never set foot there, I could still describe it, right down to the souvenir tea set from Uzbekistan in the china cabinet.

By then, Faina was pretty much over her astonishment at meeting an American who spoke Russian. I think she coped with the oddity of it, as many do, by deciding that I was somehow not quite American. Perhaps she told herself some story in which my grandparents had stayed on—I'd told her they were originally from Lithuania—miraculously surviving both world wars and the other onslaughts to die just a few blocks from here on *their* foldout couch, opposite *their* matched sets of the Russian classics, the books' spines still as stiff as the day they'd come off the press. (And yes, my grandparents' books would have been in Russian too, for they would have traded up after the war, like everyone else: out with Yiddish, in with Russian. But what am I saying? This happened in America too. What language am I writing in right now? And what language have I had to learn in a classroom, unable to master it because almost the only way to be immersed now would be to run away and join the Hasidim?)

And I had learned that Faina was a retired professor of education who volunteered at the local Jewish Museum that had risen from the ashes of the Soviet Union. She was racing against time to interview Jewish survivors while a few of them were still living; they were, she said wryly, even older and frailer than she was. She filled cassettes with their accounts of hiding in attics and barns, of sleeping rough in the forest, and waging guerilla warfare against the Germans. She was no trained historian, almost nobody at the museum was, most of them women in their seventies or eighties like her, retired from other professions — engineering, medicine, academia — who had thrown themselves into this work just as soon as the Soviet Union dried up and blew away.

For decades, she said pensively, we lived in silence with the knowledge of what had happened during the war, to our community, to our families. And while it might seem hellish to spend your days pondering the unspeakable brutality that took place here so recently, for us it's been a relief to break that oppressive silence. I've had opportunities to leave this place and live out my days in a normal country, you know — drawing herself up to her full height as she said this, she was still far from tall, but impressive nonetheless — but I need to stay here and do this work.

She nodded resolutely, as if arguing with someone only she could see.

She couldn't wait to get to the museum each day. Her husband said she was obsessed. He held down the home front, thank goodness, shopped and cooked and brought her meals. Not just lunch. Dinner too. He ate alongside her at her desk, then carried the dirty dishes home.

Here she smiled apologetically at her unseen interlocutor.

As we exited the living room, she placed a finger over her lips. He's sleeping down the hall, she said softly, leading me past a closed door and into the tiny kitchen. I paused on the threshold as she switched on a light, struck a match, and put the kettle on. This room was familiar too.

This is the apartment where I grew up from the age of twelve, she said, with a sweep of the arm that was almost grand. We came to Vilnius after the war, when I was nine, and got on the waiting list for an apartment right away. It took just three years. Just my mother and me, she said. My father died when I was two. Mine was a fatherless generation . . . How did we manage?

She seemed to be addressing herself to the tree outside the window. With a sorrowful expression, she answered her own question: we raised ourselves.

He died of an illness, my mother told me when I was very young. I believed her, though in those days war and hunger were the main killers. Against such efficient rivals, few illnesses could compete. But my mother was my authority. She struggled unceasingly to keep us alive.

Faina poured some tea to see if it had steeped, filled both cups, then rolled back a piece of cheesecloth covering a jar and scooped purplish-black jam onto tiny saucers. We dipped into it with pointed silver spoons. The seeds crunched between our teeth.

But when I grew older and could appreciate her strength and her ability to keep going after losing everything and everyone—*almost* everyone, she corrected herself with a wry smile—at that same time, I began to notice that nearly every time she mentioned my father's death, the story changed. In one version, he died in a freak accident, falling and hitting his head on the pavement while breaking up a fight between two men outside a tavern. When someone we knew died of a heart attack, that's what had killed my father too. And that time, remembering yet another version from long before, I said thoughtlessly, didn't you say he died from a stroke?

At my question, continued Faina, my mother grew hysterical. She let out unearthly shrieks. Not directed at me; I didn't feel attacked, just mystified.

I went for help. Our next-door neighbor was a nurse. She calmed my mother, gave her valerian drops, and had her lie down. Take deep breaths, the neighbor said over and over, until my mother obeyed. Two nights and a day she slept. I called her office to say she wouldn't be coming in.

After that, she didn't mention my father for nearly three years. It was as if he had abandoned us.

Faina now seemed to emerge briefly from a trance. Tell Jessica my story when you go back to America, she said. Remember everything I'm saying. I tried to tell her when she was here, but my English is poor. I don't think she understood.

I nodded. I'll tell Jessica, I said.

The matter of her story's transmission across numerous borders and an ocean now settled to her apparent satisfaction, she continued. You see, she said, my parents were Litvaks, Lithuanian Jews, but they went to Birobidjan, which is where I was born. I was born in the thirties. In the Soviet Union. Of all the centuries and countries to be born into!

It would have been better to be alive during the Spanish Inquisition, she said after a pause. We would merely have been stripped of everything we had and forced to leave the country, which would have been better than being stripped of everything and forced to stay, as we were. Strangely, though, I had a happy childhood. Everything coexisted in my mind. Stalin was our kind, jolly Soviet father.

The worst part, she said with a strangled laugh—I just remembered this, I haven't thought about it in years—is that before my parents met, my father actually went to the United States. He lived in Brooklyn for a year. That's near New York, isn't it? But he didn't like America—too materialistic, he said.

She gulped some tea, and again she laughed that mirthless laugh.

You've heard of Birobidjan, of course?

I nodded.

It was supposed to be our alternative to Palestine, she said. A Jewish homeland, right here, tucked inside the Soviet Union. Swamps and mosquitoes, as far as the eye could see. So . . . we spent the war years there, safe, very safe, yes, very far from the front— it's near China, you know—and when the Nazis retreated, we set forth for Lithuania, Mother and I. To find her family.

We stopped over in Yalta, on the Black Sea. My father's parents had fled there during the war. My mother knew the address by heart. She knocked. The door opened a crack. It was chained. An elderly woman peered out. "Wait," she said. She stepped away, then returned and thrust a bundle of letters through the narrow opening.

That was my sole glimpse of my paternal grandmother. My mother had written to this woman and her husband faithfully after my father died, thinking that her in-laws would want news of me. There was never a reply. It was wartime—maybe her let- ters weren't reaching them? But they *had* been getting through. I have that bundle still.

My mother didn't seem much surprised by her mother-in-law's reception. Decades later, when I found out about my father, I understood: we carried a vile contagion.

Three weeks it had taken us to get that far, and several changes of train. We'd spent our last kopeck. We stood in the street, a small woman with a very small child and one battered suitcase, also not large. Across the street, a light went on. Someone raised a window and called out. We went toward the voice.

We lived with that woman and her husband and baby for the better part of a year. At night, they hung a sheet across the room for privacy. They became family. Our Ukrainian family. I'm still in touch with their daughter.

My mother took in sewing, and I went to school. When we had the money saved, we set out again. The train pulled away, and we waved and waved to our friends on the platform until they disappeared from view. A few hours later, we unpacked the lunch basket. They had hidden banknotes for us in the sandwiches.

In Kovno, we went to the old neighborhood. The house was charred. No one there to greet us. Again, we stood in the street, unsure where to go.

A woman came out of a nearby house, her fair hair pulled tightly into a bun.

"Looking for your family?" she asked. "Dead. All dead."

"My sisters?" exclaimed my mother. "My parents?" she said, placing a hand on her collarbone.

"All of them," said the woman. "There were seven of you girls, weren't there? I couldn't always tell all of you apart, with your dark, frizzy hair." She waved her hands around her head to indicate a disordered mop.

My mother stood very still.

"The locals helped the Germans, I guess everyone knows that by now," said the woman. "I tried not to get involved. You never know who's going to end up in charge, you know? Would you like to know who did it?" She stared fixedly at one of the houses.

"No," my mother said, drawing out the word.

"A few of you people have come back," said the neighbor woman, tearing her gaze from the house. "Those who had the good fortune to be away when the Germans came. I say to everyone who comes back: if you like, I can tell you who killed your people. I remember it all. Some were marched away to the forest. Others were gunned down in their front yards."

There was a long silence.

The woman turned and went inside.

We went to Vilnius.

The city was abuzz with people who had moved there from all over the Soviet Union and the new factories going up. There were vast, empty lots where the bombed-out buildings had been cleared away. People were pleased: it meant more green space and more sunlight. But the wait for an apartment was still much shorter than elsewhere in the USSR. There were many empty apartments—so many people had been killed. We were allotted a room, and my mother found work as a bookkeeper. I enrolled in school and quickly mastered Lithuanian.

The Great Synagogue had been destroyed in the bombing. Just a few low walls left standing. When we arrived, a few survivors were still coming to pray among the ruins. Then the authorities tore down what remained. Well, it was a hazard. It could have collapsed at any moment. They didn't rebuild. Yes, the Soviet Union was an atheist state, but this was a practical decision. There just weren't enough Jews left to justify the expense. The country needed industry and schools. It needed hospitals.

The light was just beginning to spread across the sky again as I passed the mulberry trees.

I was in college when Khrushchev gave his secret speech, Faina continued two days later. We were in a small office at the museum. In the room were a battered abacus, several typewriters with various alphabets, and an odd-looking device that must have been some kind of early Soviet computer. Books on the history of the Jews lined the walls in Russian, Yiddish, Lithuanian, Polish, Belarusian, English, German, Hebrew. There were also books in languages and scripts I didn't recognize.

Two cups of tea steamed on the table.

That was when we learned, officially learned, she said, though there had been whispers before, that Stalin was *not* our kind, jolly father. Classes were canceled, and there was a general meeting and discussion. Our instructors wept and so did we.

Let me tell you what we heard at the college today, I said to my mother when I came home. Did you hear what Khrushchev said?

There'd been a meeting at her workplace too, of course. The whole country had interrupted their work to listen and discuss.

I heard nothing new today, my mother said with preternatural calm. She bit her lip. Then she covered her face with her hands. She sat that way for a long time.

You know, your father did not die a natural death, she said finally, looking up.

I wanted to change the subject. But there was no other subject.

He was executed, she continued. As an enemy of the people.

Why did you never tell me?

I wanted you to have a happy childhood, she said, the tears coming now. I always meant to tell you. Always. But not yet.

She gripped my sleeve. She begged my forgiveness.

Mama, I forgive you everything, I said again and again.

The whole story, everything she knew, came spilling out. It consisted mainly of gaps and conjecture. She was certain that he was guilty of nothing. He'd been accused of sabotage and wrecking, something like that, like millions of others. Maybe he'd told a joke about Stalin. Which would have been unbelievably foolish. But still.

A few months after they took him, my mother told me, she received a letter saying that he'd been sentenced to twenty-five years. Everyone knew what that meant: he would be executed, perhaps already had been. Then the mailman returned the possessions she'd hastily gathered and thrust into his hands as his new keepers led him over the threshold and away. Return of the prisoner's possessions was also widely understood as a death announcement.

Faina paused.

After the end of the Soviet Union, she continued, I flew to Siberia. All of the records for a vast swath of the Far East were consolidated in the municipal archives at Khabarovsk. My father's file was not thick, but it took me several days to get through it. I would read half a page and pause for an hour. Or notice I'd been staring at the dust motes and have no idea how long I'd been doing that.

Finally, the archivists threw me out; they needed my seat. Huge numbers of people were applying to read their relatives' files, or their own. Not all requests were granted, of course.

My father's file contained his execution date, which was just a few days after his arrest. The person who had denounced him would, a few years later, become my beloved first-grade teacher. My mother was long dead by the time I read the file. She never knew who was responsible. She had cordial relations with that person, met with him for parent-teacher conferences.

My father had been a teacher at the high school. Maybe the man wanted my father's job?

But he didn't get it. He stayed back in the first grade.

I saw Faina several more times during my remaining weeks in Lithuania. She did not return to her life story, but it was with us each time we met, like a third person at the table.

Please tell Jessica, she said before I left. Tell Jessica my story.

I'll tell Jessica, I assured her.

PART 2

The trip to Lithuania nearly a year behind me now, I was immersed once again in the quotidian: job, commute, laundry. Faina and I emailed a few times after I came back to New York. But the Cyrillic keyboard differs from our familiar qwertyuiop, and the unaccustomed stretching hurts my hands and makes my brain throb. Our correspondence foundered.

I'm coming to Chicago to visit a friend, she said when finally she called. Arkady was originally from Russia, and for some years before hopscotching over to the United States, he had lived in Lithuania in order to record the stories of that country's last surviving Jews. He's a gifted writer, she added. He's written fourteen books.

She suspected that he was very ill. He had evaded her probing questions, and when she grew more insistent, had replied serenely that God would take care of him. God, indeed! said Faina to me on the phone. Arkady and his wife were *baal teshuvah*, Jewish-born returnees to the faith, and they took their Judaism very seriously, while Faina was an ordinary Soviet Jew, remote from all considerations of the divine. She had decided to come over and see for herself how things stood with her friend.

I doubt I'll be going to Lithuania again, I said to myself as I hung up. I'd spent sufficient time in that killing field my mother's parents had once called home. I'd better see Faina while she's on this side of the ocean; she's frail; it will be the last time we meet.

I advanced through this series of realizations as if working out a proof.

———————

Arkady and his wife lived in a high-rise close to Lake Michigan. Everything in the apartment was white: kitchen cabinets, leather furniture, wall-to-wall carpets. There was an immense flat-screen television. The windows stretched floor to ceiling. All day, we sat at an immense table, eating and talking.

The food: whitefish salad, lox, tuna salad, herring, something called Israeli salad with tomatoes, cucumbers, and dill. Baklava.

The talk: I remember little, except that as we spoke, history sat off to the side, glowering like a large, angry dog. I speak Russian fluently, yes, I'm right there as the conversation unspools, a full participant, but I immediately forget a great deal, chunks just break off and float away. Cognition is a zero sum game, is how I

explain this to myself: the additional effort required to compre-
hend and formulate in a foreign language is subtracted from the
capacity for recall. When it's over, you run a search on your rec-
ollections only to realize that the conversation has left shockingly
few traces. When you leave your native language, you breathe a
different substance, and like a mermaid who comes ashore, you
cannot comfortably stay for long. Your native depths keep calling
you home.

The host did look as if something was terribly wrong, but if
Faina had not mentioned his illness, I would simply have thought:
here is another life shattered by immigration, nothing more. It's
much worse for the men. If they land here after forty, there's no
way to repair the damage.

He asked what books I'd translated, and I mentioned the one
about the events leading up to the Night of the Murdered Poets.
Arkady knew of the events and was even familiar with the terrible
and little-known descriptor.

One way to frame the destruction of European Jewry is that
Hitler killed the readers of Yiddish literature. And one August
night in 1952, Stalin did the complementary deed, killing many
of its writers, assuring thereby the near-extinction of an entire
literature. But for the fact that they were on opposite sides of the
war, you might think that they had planned this literary genocide
together, so neatly do its parts dovetail.

Just before I left to fly back to New York, Arkady produced three
copies of his book, each one inscribed, a different inscription in
each book, each one addressed to me and bearing his signature
and the date. Two were the Russian originals, and one was the
German translation. I cannot read German, and I was clear about
this, but he was simply throwing everything he had my way. He
asked me to read the book, adding proudly that in addition to the

German translation, there were now translations into Hebrew, Lithuanian, and Spanish. The critics who had read it in translation had loved it, every last one of them. But this meant little to him as long as there was no English version.

Let's nip this in the bud right now, I thought, and I said to him, I don't translate anymore, except at my job, and that's just routine stuff, correspondence, treaties, and reports, and much more French than Russian. No more literary translation: I've chosen to write instead. He nodded, but with his fourteen books I could see that he just didn't get that someone might have difficulty sitting down to write.

But I'll be happy to read it, I added.

———

Arkady, his wife, and Faina waved vigorously as the airport van pulled away.

"Is that lady your mother?" the driver asked me.

"Which one?" I asked, although my mother was several states away.

"With the red scarf."

"She's my friend."

"She loves you very much, that lady. She looked," he said, shifting up, "as if seeing you leave now was the worst thing that ever happened to her."

"No," I said. "She's seen worse."

———

I hurtled shivering through the mists, O'Hare back to LaGuardia. In the brief intervals between dreams, my mind said over and over: the human body was not made to travel at such speeds. Slumped against the window, I could almost feel the damp on the other side of the thick pane seeping into me.

I clutched the book. I'd put two of them in my bag and kept

out one copy to hold on the plane, as a talisman. Sleep told me that if my grip on that book loosened, the plane would plummet from the sky.

On the cover was a drawing of a human being from the waist up, with large, panicked eyes in a small face and massive, pale hands outstretched. The figure was sinking into an indeterminate black mass flecked with white, which might be a pile of leaves or straw, or possibly a fanciful representation of a snowdrift by night. The little creature was slipping inexorably into an engulfing darkness, some cataclysm that was no doubt explained within.

———————

The man who was the focus of the book (Russian speakers always say "hero," but often, and certainly in this case, there is little heroism involved, and so the word is best rendered in English as "protagonist") was one of Arkady's interview subjects in Vilnius. In the 1990s, the protagonist, Kazimeras, as I will call him (a venerable Lithuanian name for a man, meaning "great destroyer"), was dying of congestive heart failure. He was wearisome to himself, if not downright hateful, and glad that he would soon shake himself off.

At their first session, he greeted the younger man without rising. With the blanket spread over his lap, he was nonetheless impressive. "I am the last living Lithuanian Yiddish poet," he intoned. In fact, he had murdered the Yiddish poet in himself decades before. I'm getting to that.

———————

For three or four years, Arkady went to Kazimeras's home to interview him several mornings a week. The dying man had been a Yiddish poet and man of letters before the war. His work bore the influence of the Russians, whom he loved. Quintessentially of the borderlands, he was also steeped in the German idealists and the works of Adam Mickiewicz, the national poet of Poland. His essays and poetry ran in Lithuania's most prestigious Yiddish periodicals—there were many excellent venues then; Yiddish literary culture flourished there before the war. He made his living as a newspaperman.

The book began in the small Lithuanian town where his father had owned a thriving enterprise that produced ladies' accessories: scarves, lingerie, stockings, that sort of thing. His parents had provided a decent religious education. At home, they spoke only Yiddish.

At age fifteen, he fell in love, if you want to call it that, with a gentile girl. They trysted in an abandoned Jewish cemetery. Just as the nights were getting cooler and they were wondering where to go now, the boy's father learned of his liaison and, roaring with rage, insisted that he break it off. An obedient son, Kazimeras passed the girl in the street without speaking.

He learned later, he told Arkady, that during the war she'd been held for many months by the Germans, raped over and over. Collateral damage: the usual wartime stuff. She turned to drink after her release, ending up in some sort of institution.

In Vilnius (after the war, the city went only by its Lithuanian name), he also passed her on the street. She must have been allowed out of the institution sometimes, or maybe from time to time she would make a brief escape. Her face had been ravaged by drink. Her features seemed to drip down her face; her mouth looked like a twisted, throbbing wound. Although she was nearly unrecognizable, she was now the one who did not appear to see him.

I'm recounting the events out of order, as they come to me. It's some time since I read the book, so I don't vouch for the accuracy of my retelling.

This next part is important. When the Nazis came to Lithuania, our protagonist was detained at a checkpoint. He persuaded his captors to release him, which happened more often than you might think: they were human beings too, strange as it is to say that now, but in the course of it all, he let slip his family's address.

He didn't return to the family house after that. He went straight to the recruitment office and from there to the front. He kept writing to the family at the old address. He explained that he'd gone to fight in the war. He didn't hear back. After the war, he confirmed, in a pro forma kind of way, that his family was gone, disappeared. Like almost everyone he'd known. His letters probably too.

At the front, he continued writing Yiddish poems and kept them in his boots. Some he memorized and didn't write down at all. But, returning to Vilnius after the war, he learned that all of the Yiddish publications were gone—there was no one left to write for them, no one left to put them out, and worst of all, no one left to read them.

In the newly Sovietized Lithuania, it was not safe to be a Yiddish writer. Not safe to be a Yiddish writer? Good God, it was not safe to be a Jew. The Nazis had been vanquished, but their strain of contagion had survived and mingled with the native anti-Semitism, and the hardy hybrid was spreading.

He changed his name to something that sounded more Lithuanian. He worked to improve his grasp of that language. First, he hired someone to translate his Yiddish writings into Lithuanian, and he studied the translations in minute detail. Next, he translated his work himself and had his Lithuanian edited until it read like the work of a native, or nearly so. Finally, he ceased writing in Yiddish altogether, working directly into Lithuanian. Imagine translations for which no original exists.

He decided that he would become a playwright. Writers for the stage don't need to know the language perfectly, he told Arkady. The actors provide the final polish in rehearsal as they make the words their own.

He thought his literary self-improvement project was done, until he realized with horror that if he continued to read his beloved Yiddish writers, he was ensuring that his Lithuanian would retain that same Yiddish lilt he was struggling to eradicate. There was only one way to make himself stop.

He did it by night, when the maid was gone and the family was asleep. It took many nights. The furnace choked and sputtered; he was in too much of a rush. The smoke was very black and the ash got everywhere: in his nose, his mouth. It was a new way of consuming Yiddish literature.

One book, though. . . . It was a sacred text. A birthday gift. From a poet, a man more talented than he by far. The poet had been swept up in the wave of anti-Jewish persecutions with which the Soviets marked the war's end. The most Kazimeras could do was tear out the flyleaf where the giver had written an inscription in Yiddish. The page bore the imprisoned man's name and his own, his real name, the one he'd published under before the war. That page was a death sentence if his house was ever searched, a death sentence for him *and* his friend, if the friend survived his current sentence, whereas the book by itself with the page gone was worth just a few years of imprisonment. Everyone was an expert now at sentences—at what offenses resulted in what punishments. The book, he kept.

As he ripped out the page with the inscription, he remembered a small thing he loved about his mother tongue: Yiddish has two words for "book": German *buch* for a secular work, Hebrew *sefer* for holy texts. Not even related—two different categories of thing. Is there any other language that makes such a distinction? he asked himself, with mingled pride and shame.

Day after day, he passed the poet's wife on the stairs at the Writers Union. She worked as a typist; someone with clout had helped her to hang on to the job after her husband disappeared. If he greeted her, what would he say? He might find himself asking if she had word of her husband, if she knew his whereabouts. Or if there was anything she needed: Food? Something for the children? They were very young.

Better not to start; he could do nothing. He maintained silence.

Years later, the poet returned. It was the time of the Thaw. The disappeared were coming home—those who had survived. Kazimeras and his wife could invite the couple over for dinner now, they decided. The poet's wife greeted him warmly. Kazimeras understood: she didn't want her husband to know. Plus, if she gave the cold shoulder now to everyone who had ignored her when her husband was in exile, there would be no one to talk to. She understood why people had shunned her and didn't take it personally.

Late in the evening, the two men were discussing some fine point of the faith in which neither of them believed any longer, some question that had preoccupied them at the study house before the war. His friend glanced over at the shelves and asked to consult his gift.

"Of course!" the host exclaimed. He rose and went to pull down the book; though he hadn't taken it down in years, he knew exactly where it was. Only, he forgot, for just a moment, about the missing flyleaf.

"Oh," he said, letting his hand drop, "it must be upstairs." He made no move to go there.

———————

And so it went, down the decades, with betrayal following on betrayal, small ones, larger ones, and because he had an unerring instinct for self-preservation, they were always appropriate to the political moods and current events, which shifted and replaced each other like theatrical sets gliding on an invisible track. Despite his bumpy Lithuanian, he achieved success as a playwright. As a member of the Writers Union, he had privileges. A car. A modest country house. Fresh strawberries in winter. A bottle of French brandy a few times a year.

Lines had to be cut sometimes, scenes rewritten. He learned to do this rapidly so that premieres were not postponed. He figured out how to avoid the authorities' attention. An incendiary comment could get through if placed in the mouth of an unsavory character, someone who was dark, foreign, had a lisp, an accent, or a bad leg.

As he aged, the words came more slowly, just as they had early on, when he was learning to write in Lithuanian. When he fell ill, he stopped writing altogether. He felt he had earned his leisure and did not miss the work of writing; the love of writing had left when he cast out Yiddish. He continued to attend rehearsals when his plays were revived. He approved alternate wordings when the actors had difficulty fitting their mouths around his lines.

It was around the time he became too weak to go to the theater even a few times a week that Arkady turned up to ask questions, record his responses, and somehow (Kazimeras himself did not see how it could be done) fashion it all into a book. The timing was felicitous. His writing was not immortal, Kazimeras knew that, but there were some things he needed to say.

The interviews were conducted in Russian; Arkady, despite his professional interest in writers who worked in other languages, was monolingual. Russian was a stretch for Kazimeras; it was his third language, and his accent was very strong. But his will was stronger still. Whatever language the circumstances required, he would bend it to his needs.

I raced through most of the book right after I got back from Chicago; then, uncharacteristically, I set it aside with the last ten pages unread, for it belonged to my encounter with Arkady. For months, it lay forgotten among the thousands of books in my small apartment, shelved with my small but growing collection on Jewish Lithuania and on Vilne (that's the Yiddish name for the city, which has fallen into disuse), known as the Jerusalem of the North: works of history, volumes on its architecture and on its Jewish ghetto.

Next to these were my books on and in the Yiddish language: Yiddish poetry, Yiddish poetry in translation, Yiddish-English dictionaries, a Yiddish-French dictionary, books on the history of the language, born of the encounter between German, Hebrew, Aramaic, Ukrainian, and Polish. And Yiddish grammar books, many grammar books: for grammar is the skeleton, words merely the flesh that pads it out. No one who is ignorant of the grammar of a language can claim knowledge of that language. And grammar is violent; it is about who is doing what to whom, and so it must be grasped and wrestled to the ground. My brain was weary from language learning; this time around I hoped that mere possession of grammar books would lead osmotically to mastery.

———————

"You're very well connected in the New York literary world," said the quavery voice. "Jim told me."

A pause followed.

"He says you're a literary agent."

The subtext: *You didn't tell me these things yourself back when we met. And how come you never mentioned that you know Jim?*

We were speaking Russian; Arkady had been settled in Chicago for over a decade, but he'd come to the US too late in life to master English.

I barely knew Jim. Jim was a Russian professor at a university in Arkansas; we'd met once at a Slavic Studies conference. Jim had said that I was well connected in the literary world? That I was an agent? I didn't believe he'd said these things, but neither did I think that Arkady was a liar. He believed what he was telling me, believed with the desperation and fierce faith of an immigrant.

I suppressed a sigh. Did a few book translations published more than a dozen years ago make me well connected? A sheaf of honorable mentions in literary competitions unknown beyond a coterie of judges and entrants? The occasional story in a literary magazine out of Oklahoma or Oregon? I'd heard that literary talent scouts read those magazines, but none had ever contacted me.

The Book of Disaster, Arkady's book was called. If he succeeded in finding a translator and a publisher (he thought I could make this happen), the title might change, as titles often do in translation. In English, it might be called something like *The Suicide That Took Fifty Years*.

I just made that one up. But it fits.

I don't remember now when the calls began. Probably the first one came in the fall, just before the holiest season, some six months after my trip to Chicago. *L'shana tova*, he said, and I repeated the syllables back to him. He was calling to wish me a sweet year.

He asked whether I had read the book, what I thought of it, and—what I had said in Chicago had made no impression— whether I would consider doing the English translation and helping him place it. He also spoke of the travails of attracting an American publisher.

Our conversations had a desultory, almost hopeless quality. Fragmentary utterances emerged out of long pauses and faded away into ellipses. He referred haltingly to his illness.

On one call, he blurted out that he and his wife had gone to a rabbi in Brooklyn right after he was diagnosed, some five years earlier. I knew that this particular rabbi was held in certain quarters to be the Messiah and that there were always petitioners at his door: barren women, abandoned wives, people who had forgotten that suffering is inevitable, even though they heard the Book of Job read out year after year in the synagogue.

He and his wife were not followers of the rabbi, Arkady

hastened to explain, though they owned all of his DVDs and watched them quite often now. A visit to him could not hurt, they had told themselves. If Arkady's condition had continued to deteriorate afterward, why, that had nothing to do with the messiah of Brooklyn. Without the rabbi's intercession, his health might have declined even faster.

Sometimes he called right after he'd been discharged from the hospital following a severe bout. Sometimes he apologized for missing the previous Jewish holiday, whichever one it was, explaining that his condition at the time had prevented him from calling. When he didn't mention his illness, it was nonetheless present in the weakness of his voice.

A world in which people called on the holidays to say *gut yontif* was utterly foreign to me. Now I noted when the holidays fell and when the call did not come, I noted that too.

As Arkady continued to call, I was for the first time strongly tempted to take on the translation, and not only because to do so would help ease his passage through his illness. The bizarre, devastating story of the last Lithuanian Yiddish poet and his moral decay absorbed me deeply. I hadn't read the last pages, I now understood, because I was afraid of the end.

To translate *The Book of Disaster* would keep me involved in Jewish life for as long as I labored over it, and if it was published and my name appeared somewhere on it, my residual involvement would last as long as the book had readers, even as long as it existed as a physical object. Absorption in the work would provide respite from the thorny question of what it means to be a Jew who is not at home with the rituals and the prayers, allowing me to concentrate on the recent, profane history of the Jews that is documented, rather than the ancient, sacred history that is a matter of faith.

But I did not grasp the book in the deep and complete way that a translator must. There were two first-person narrators, and which "I" was speaking was not always clear to me. I could simply hew closely to the original and leave the reader to guess as well. But would that be right? And how would I reproduce subtle differences in the way the two men spoke when I wasn't sure that I was always alert to those differences?

One of the most difficult tasks a translator faces is to stay faithful when what is going on is deliberately left unclear. This was a book marked by inconclusiveness and ambiguity. Presented with a confusing array of possible outcomes, or none at all, the translator must resist the binary choice, if none is given, setting down the words that will leave the reader in the dark. I feared I lacked the fortitude for this.

The calls continued.

Following that conversation when he gently insinuated that I'd been holding out on him, I began to get ideas about who might take an interest. There was a boutique house in Indiana that specialized in Kafka-inflected works by obscure geniuses from countries like Albania and Turkmenistan. I had turned down a two-book translation deal from them. There was a one-woman publisher in Woodstock who issued translations on rice paper, with woodcuts. I had stood next to an author of hers at the podium during a literary festival, translating his remarks. An Inuit from the Russian Far North, he had likened himself and the other writers on the panel to a team of sled dogs.

I urged Arkady to get in touch with these publishers. His wife, whose English was good, could help him clear the language barrier. I would put in a word with the people I knew. Both houses must certainly have established working relationships with good translators.

They just might be interested.

He kept on calling me.

———

Now I remembered the press that had brought out my translation of the book about the murdered poets. The director was no longer in publishing; in the decade since I had translated my last book, he had somehow made the leap to heading a Jewish historical archive and research institute. But he had maintained ties with his old place of work, and I'd heard that the research institute and the press sometimes collaborated on special projects.

The package I assembled would have made a publicist proud. A cover letter, in which I congratulated the former publisher on his career change and captured the premise of *The Book of Disaster* in a few pithy paragraphs; a four-sentence author bio and a page of ecstatic quotes from the reviews of the Russian, German, and Hebrew editions, courtesy of Arkady; beneath that, an English translation of the book's opening pages, done at my urging by Jim the Slavic studies professor, after I wrote and reminded him who I was. Jim's translation resume went into the package too, as did the German edition of the book and one of the Russian ones.

I pushed the bulging envelope across the counter at the post office. I've done everything I can, I told myself; this is out of my hands now.

My expectations were low. I remembered the former publisher, a small man with a quiff of black hair and an air of supreme confidence, as someone with numerous claims on his time. I knew of writers who had withdrawn accepted manuscripts from his house in despair and gone to other, far less prestigious publishers when months and months of unreturned phone calls became too much to bear.

Arkady was pleased when I told him where I'd sent the book. He knew the man's name. Without meaning to, I had confirmed his suspicions: yes, I was well connected; yes, I had been holding out on him.

PART 3

By the time I put the package in the mail, I'd been haunting the Archive for some time. I did not go there to do research; I am no scholar.

The Archive is home to historic pieces of paper of all kinds—a great diversity of papers that I imagine all slumbering and keeping each other warm beneath their shared blanket of dust: records of births, marriages, divorces and deaths; maps; letters, diaries, and photographs of people accomplished and ordinary; manuscripts by thinkers and writers from all points along the obscurity/fame continuum; elementary school compositions by pupils who would now be more than a century old; newspapers and magazines from across the region known as Yiddishland; scratchy recordings of itinerant wedding bands, interviews with village women about spells cast and curses laid, and scholars discoursing on philosophy and philology during fundraising dinners (with the sounds of clattering china and utensils coming through); theater handbills; also, shopping lists, recipes, advertising circulars, instruction manuals for home appliances, and dress patterns on crumbling tissue paper—such things are historic too, if old enough, and especially if written in Yiddish—for this archive is no mere Jewish archive, it is a *Yiddish* archive. (This Jewish/Yiddish distinction is one that few languages permit; in many languages, including Yiddish itself, there is a single word that means both "Jewish" and "Yiddish," making the Yiddish language into "the Jewish language," although there are, of course, many Jewish languages that are not Yiddish, not at all, such as Haketia, Karaim, Kayla, Krymchak, Shuadit, and Zarphatic, to name some of the lesser-known ones.)

But in addition to housing these important scraps, the Archive regularly opens its doors to the public for a range of events, from a talk about a diary kept by someone in the anti-Nazi guerilla underground in Poland that was recently discovered in the diarist's grandson's attic crawl space in Hoboken; to talks on the nexus of Yiddish jokes and Freudian psychoanalysis and the legend of the dybbuk, a spirit believed to possess Jewish girls dying of unrequited love or forced into arranged marriages; and on the golem, a creature native to Prague and shaped out of clay from its river banks, whose makers would give it life by whispering into one clay ear the word *emet*, Hebrew for "truth," its purpose to kill and maim the oppressors of the Jews, but who, its task completed, might continue ruthlessly, mechanically killing whoever or whatever crossed its path (dogs, Jews), until it was itself sliced to bloody bits and disabled, often by the same fearless rabbi who had animated it. The Archive hosted a staged reading of a play called *Money, Love, and Shame*, billed as "a wildly popular trashy melodrama from the Yiddish theater." On one occasion, Philip Roth emerged from seclusion to discuss his oeuvre at the Archive.

In days gone by, Jews recently arrived from the Old Country would found or join *landsmanshaftn*, known blandly in English as "compatriots' associations," with "compatriot'" meant here in the narrowest sense, referring to people from particular towns rather than entire countries. People who hailed from the same dot on the map of Bohemia, Podolia, Trancarpathia, Transnistria, or Volhynia would gather in rented halls to celebrate the holidays, to raise funds for each other's medical or legal emergencies and burials, or to make matches between their children, whom they optimistically considered among the few known quantities in the strange new land. By the time of this story, the *landsmanshaftn* were mostly defunct, though a few were still on life support, responsibility for them having been passed down to the founders' aging children or grandchildren, many of whom had never seen the towns they commemorated.

Despite its ambitious scholarly mission as the national academy of letters for this language without a country, the Archive was for me something more like a *landsmanschaft*. Founded in Vilne in the early twentieth century, later it (or much of its collection) had been carefully packed into thousands of boxes and whisked over to New York City one jump ahead of the Nazis. Some of the Archive's holdings had been hidden deep in the Lithuanian earth during the war, hidden so well that after the war ended, some items were never found. These things left behind made the

Archive even more of a bridge across time, more of a place to seek the lost, the familiar.

At the Archive events, there are always people I know in the audience: former Yiddish classmates and teachers, along with other pillars of the Yiddish community, including Yiddish actors, singers, translators, folklorists, amateur lexicographers, and professional poets' widows. Often I feel the urge to flee at evening's end without exchanging a word with any of them. It's because I'm supposed to speak to them in Yiddish — for how will the language survive unless everyone speaks it who can speak it at all, even badly, even barely, and where will we speak it, if not at the Archive, the closest thing this homeless language has to a home?

But despite my years of classes and my love for the language, for the way the very sound of it renders me instantly whole, for a time, while also making me recognize just how fractured I am and helping me forgive myself for that, because, given the dislocations of Jewish history, what could be more natural than to be fractured? — despite all of that, my conversational Yiddish remains lousy. Whereas many of the people in these audiences speak a Yiddish burnished by years of constant home use and of reading beloved authors in the original, engaging in scholarly work in Yiddish linguistics or literature, singing Yiddish art songs, translating *Winnie the Pooh* into Yiddish, or designing Yiddish Scrabble sets. I am barely capable of speaking to them in Yiddish, but I can hardly speak to them in English. The remaining options are silence — or flight.

I also see there familiar faces I cannot place, probably because I've seen them nowhere else. But through repeated sightings, they take on associations. I begin to think I know them. They could be the faces of distant relatives — I believe that, I almost do. And in that connection, I think often of an early-twentieth-century immigrant and socialist I once read about who wrote in to a Yiddish newspaper to explain why he still went to shul, though he had long since ceased to believe in God: his friends and family went to the synagogue to be near God, he wrote, and he, who was without faith, without faith in God, that is, went to the synagogue to be near his friends and family.

I've concluded, after reading, thinking, and watching observant Jews at their prayers, that the existence or nonexistence of God is not central. What counts is history; story. God is merely a very, very important character in the story of the history of the Jews; he is the hero, or perhaps just the protagonist. But we are all part of the story, all characters of greater or lesser importance.

And so the Archive is also my synagogue, where I go to be present to my forbears, to the things they have written, and to the things they read.

———————

I am not yet old, but as an immigrant from the predigital era, I cannot get used to the way people respond to communications now: blindingly fast (a speed captured by the word *blitz-brivl*, Yiddish for "email") or never or in some way that manages to be both.

"Thank you so much . . . fascinating . . . ," began the reply to my package, ". . . perusing it in Russian . . ." (now I remembered that he had a doctorate in Soviet Studies) "but my time . . . sadly limited . . . would like to help . . . perhaps cosponsor in some way . . ." He asked me to call.

"Of course it would be wonderful if you translated it," he said almost immediately.

I reminded him about Jim, who had done the enclosed translation sample, saying that he was very skilled, with a strong interest in *The Disaster*, as I had come to think of it—I stopped myself just before I uttered the word, saying simply "the book"—and experience translating works on World War II and its aftermath from Russian, as well as Polish and Belarusian . . .

"Okay, well, perhaps I'll get in touch," he said, suddenly businesslike.

There was a pause.

"Hmmm . . . ," he said. "Do you feel under any kind of time pressure regarding this project?"

"*I* don't," I said. "However, the author is seriously ill. He sees publication of this book in English as . . . uh . . . his last . . . his final . . . he needs it, do you understand?"

"Hmmm . . ."

"I've no idea what the prognosis is," I added.

I continued to visit the Archive but did not go out of my way to speak to its head; why put him on the spot? Sometimes he walked past without making eye contact. Sometimes he crossed a crowded room to greet me.

"I've been spending every waking moment with *him*," he said on one occasion, gesturing toward a bulky man with a beard, who was surrounded by admirers.

"As soon as I put him on the plane tomorrow and wrap up a few things, I'll call you. Promise." Squeezing my hand, he rejoined the bearded man, leaving me to a precarious heap of pineapple chunks on a small paper plate.

It was a reception—lavish, by Archive standards—to honor the bearded man, who had just delivered an endowed lecture. He had led linguistic field expeditions around Lithuania in the early aughts, recording the last surviving native speakers of Yiddish. He had mapped the invisible borders where dialects arise and fade into other dialects. He had noted five different Yiddish words for "potato," whose frequency of use varied by region. He had recorded regional variants—open, closed, in between—in native speakers' pronunciation of the vowel "ayin."

He and his collaborators would drive into the central square of a village, he said, spill out of their tiny car like circus clowns, and approach the first old woman they saw. The old women know everything, he said. They're the unofficial historians. We would ask if there were any Jews still in the town. Oh yes, there's one left, the woman might say, pointing to a house. We would knock.

One place we went, there was an enormous cross on the mantelpiece. And the man, he didn't know his wife was Jewish. They'd been married fifty years and she'd never mentioned it. She kept casting nervous glances his way as we set up the recording equipment.

When we asked her to speak Yiddish, she started apologizing. She hadn't spoken *mame-loshen* since before the war — everybody was dead. We spoke Yiddish to her for some thirty minutes, her husband glowering in the corner, and the tears flowed nonstop — hers, I mean. She kept turning to look at him and then turning back to us and answering in Lithuanian.

After half an hour or so, she began emitting a stream of the purest Yiddish you've ever heard. Lovely, early twentieth-century Yiddish, with none of the contemporary Russian, Polish, or Lithuanian impurities that slip in when someone is having memory lapses because there aren't enough people around who speak their language.

Boy, her husband was not pleased. He couldn't understand a word, of course. I don't like to imagine what transpired after we left. He was a beefy guy, red-faced. Looked like a heavy drinker.

———

The last of the many fieldwork stories that evening concerned a young Jewish girl sheltered by a Lithuanian farm family during the war — devout Catholics, of course.

One time, they asked her to come downstairs. It was safe, they said, no one was around, no Germans, and none of the local Jew-haters either. She emerged from her hiding place.

They sprinkled some water on her head. For some reason, this made all the whole family very happy. If they were happy, she was happy; they were saving her life, and for that she was infinitely grateful.

Not until after the war did she learn what those drops of water meant: they meant that she was not Jewish any more. The people who had saved her from being killed as a Jew had turned her into a Christian.

There had been two Jewish men who wanted to marry her when she was young, but when she told them she'd been baptized, they both lost interest. She was old now, alone and childless. All because some Lithuanian heroes whose names were inscribed on the wall at Yad Vashem had converted her to Christianity without telling her.

Lately she'd heard that she might be able to reconvert. The old Jewish cemetery had recently been cleaned up and reopened. She needed to act quickly so she could be buried there. But there was now only one rabbi for all of Lithuania. He said he would try to make it to her village.

She feared she might die first.

———

At the Archive that evening, the atmosphere was electric. Those stories about being the last of a kind, about outliving a world, awoke something in everyone present. Each of us has something that will die with us; we all carry within us smithereens of the past; we all come from somewhere only dimly recalled. Someone is the last Yiddish speaker in the village; someone is the last Yiddish poet in the country; the rest of us are the last of something we can barely name. As in that most famous Hasidic story of them all, some of us remember the prayer, some the candle, some the location of the sacred clearing where God awaits our cry for help in time of crisis. Some remember almost nothing, but are pulled along by those who do. And the fragmentary nature of remembering builds community, as people put their heads together to assemble the puzzle. Everyone holds a piece of the mystery; no one holds it all.

That evening, I felt no urge to flee. If a native Yiddish speaker needed to hear the language for thirty minutes before she could be induced to speak it, how could anyone expect me to demonstrate facility with Yiddish?

———————

The director of the Archive fell out of touch. I found another prospect: Pete the literary agent. Years ago, he'd represented a book I translated, the one on Russian obscenities and criminal slang, with the rhyming ditties. Once or twice a year, royalty checks from his office still appeared in my mailbox, most recently one for thirteen dollars and change. He'd even written a book himself, long ago; a slender volume called *Sit Down in That Chair and Write Your Blockbuster Now.*

I just made that one up. But it fits.

Every five years or so, he called to ask if there were any new books in Russian that I absolutely loved and considered a must for the American readership. Now I pitched to him for the first time. He declared himself fascinated by the story of the last Yiddish poet in Lithuania. He asked to speak with Arkady.

"Next week is out," said Pete when I tried to schedule. "I'm taking my wife to the Shakespeare Festival up in Ontario. Oh, and the week after that, I'm taking her to the country house. Upstate." *Taking her.* I envisioned him striding northward, a lissome trophy wife resting lightly in his arms.

"Give my assistant a buzz; he has my availability," he said finally.

"Whenever he's free, I can talk," said Arkady, his voice weaker than usual. "I don't usually make important decisions during *bein hametzarim*," he told me. But three weeks from Tuesday would work, immediately following his weekly treatment at the hospital.

Bein hametzarim. The three-week mourning period preceding commemoration of the destruction of the Temple, I read. During this time, religious Jews do not get their hair cut. They do not have weddings. They avoid all overt expressions of joy.

I would of course serve as the interpreter during the phone call, although I doubted my ability to bridge the chasm separating these two men; here was yet another language task destined to fail.

On the phone, Arkady expressed profound gratitude to Pete for his interest.

"You will be handsomely rewarded," he said.

I translated.

"Hey," said Pete to me in a stage whisper, "didn't you tell him how we literary agents work? He doesn't pay me; I automatically get fifteen per cent."

I conveyed this to Arkady.

"You will be richly rewarded," he repeated.

"My dear," Pete said with a chuckle, "tell him he's got a successful literary agent on the line. I can afford to take on the occasional project that is not profitable."

I complied.

"You are a truly noble man," said Arkady.

"Thanks, buddy."

A small flame of hope flared now. Pete mentioned the names of the publishers he was going to approach. He asked for a more detailed synopsis, which Arkady happily set about drafting.

Then came this: "I well understand your fascination with this extraordinary work. But I don't know who would publish it, other than a university press with a specialty in Judaica."

"And"—this next part as if he had only just thought of it—"there is, of course, the considerable expense of getting it translated."

It seemed that he had forgotten his own overtures. Had he never expressed interest, never approached the author through me, never suggested moving forward?

From my somber tone, Arkady knew as soon as he picked up that something was off. He had expected the worst; he always did. As his plaint unspooled, images of destruction flashed before me, and words came to me unbidden:

> My sighs are many,
> And my heart is sick . . .
> Delusion and folly . . .
> Delusion and deception.

How did I even know these lines? And how did I know their source — *Lamentations*?

"*The Book of Disaster* has too much pain in it for the American readership," I told Arkady the very last time we talked about his book. "You and I feel that people need to know this story, and it does capture their interest; they stop and stare. But ultimately, it repels more than it attracts. It's not saleable." I could not believe I was applying this word to *The Disaster*, even as I was struggling to say that this story could not be reduced to the notion of sales and products.

I began to fear that my attempts to bring the book to market were taking a serious toll on his health. I did not tell him this, but if his hopes were raised again, then dashed again, what would become of him? I could not continue. I stepped away from the project. Perhaps he still wonders why.

Arkady, are you struggling through this narrative right now, dictionary in hand? (You told me once that one of your fourteen books was about a nineteenth-century Lithuanian-language author, a priest if I recall, and in that connection you mentioned with

modest pride your unusual ability to gauge the talents of writers working in languages you know badly or not at all.) Arkady,
if you're reading this story, which is my story—your story—
Kazimeras's story, please know that I'm down on my knees, beg-
ging your forgiveness for this fast and loose retelling—it's the
best I can do.

Russian Afternoons

"CARPETS CLEANED, ANY SIZE," read one of the glossy slips. "Best airport car service in the city, excellent rates to JFK and LaGuardia," promised another. The packets from the neighborhood merchants association came regularly in the mail. "Hot stone back rub, chocolate body treatment, traditional massage," said the one that caught my eye. "Low prices."

Hedonism at bargain-basement rates. The combination was irresistible.

———

The receptionist who booked my appointment over the phone had that familiar accent. A few days later, I descended the stairs to the basement spa to find that women in white smocks were speaking Russian all around me.

It was the old dilemma. I do not have the flaxen-haired, sloe-eyed Slavic look; I speak English like the American that I am; should I take these industrious women off guard by addressing them in their language?

On the one hand, it seemed the courteous thing to do; I should let them know I understood, so they wouldn't talk among themselves as if I wasn't there. And if I spoke Russian with these hardworking women in their windowless world beneath the fashionable shops and cafés of Columbus Avenue, they might, for a moment anyway, feel a bit more at home amid the alienation of their workaday immigrant lives.

On the other hand, with a strong cultural us/them, Russian-versus-foreigner distinction practically built into the very structure of their language, they might grow more uneasy with me than with the other Americans they brushed up against every day, because with each Russian phrase I uttered, I would become harder and harder to classify.

And I would have to answer the wearisome questions: How did you learn Russian? (In college and in Russia/Georgia/ Uzbekistan/Siberia/Brooklyn and through books, movies, television, socializing, and the husband method—but all of this is from a different story.) What made you decide to learn Russian? (*Anna Karenina* was assigned reading in tenth grade, plus I had an adolescent craving for exotic experiences.) Come on, your parents must be Russian, right? (Wrong: Mom and Dad are monolingual Americans who grew up in Chicago and Newark, respectively.)

Sometimes I say that my mother is Russian and that I spoke Russian as a child. It's so much simpler. But not true. Sometimes I don't let on that I speak Russian and conduct the whole transaction, whatever it is, in English. Lying about my mother or dissembling about myself—I can never decide which is worse.

———

Once, a stocky cab driver picked me up at my parents' in Queens to drive me home to Manhattan. (I used to make the trip by subway, but now I get too short of breath on the stairs.) Over the radio, he chatted with his dispatcher in Ukrainian-accented Russian. So I spoke to him.

I do not do this to "practice" my Russian. I've spent too much time speaking Russian, in situations where there was too much at stake, politically or personally, or where speaking Russian was the only option, or where I was being paid for my ability to speak Russian, paid handsomely, ever to consider any conversation in Russian mere practice. Switching into Russian is about entering my interlocutor's world, a world that has been partly mine too. It's about empathy, about visiting an important but disused part of myself, and yes, about nostalgia.

By the end of the ride, I knew that he was a retired Soviet Army officer (he received his tiny military pension in depreciating Ukrainian *grivnias*, which a friend back home signed for each month and kept for him in a growing stack of shoeboxes at a dacha outside Kharkov); that he had come to America the previous year; that he was recently divorced and being supported by his sister, who, married to a real estate developer in Jersey City, had a ten-year head start on him in America. As he pulled up in front of my building, he handed back my American Express card with his car service business card tucked underneath. He asked if he could pick me up the next time I went to Queens.

"I'll remember the address by heart," he said. He seized my hand, which was still holding both cards, and pressed it to his lips.

———————

The door to the little massage room closed behind me, and the masseuse, a large-boned woman with black eyebrows and long, smooth hair the color of butter, introduced herself as Helen.

Panting slightly, I positioned myself face down on the massage table with a fluffy white towel covering my rear end. Maybe because I was naked, I decided on the direct approach.

"May I speak Russian with you?" I asked, in Russian.

Some people grow flustered at this. They pretend not to understand, respond in their best English, which is often not good, even insist that English is actually their native tongue, saying so in an English so heavily accented that it's hard to suppress a smile. It would take a far deeper understanding of Russian history and culture than I will ever possess to understand why so many Russian expatriates do not want to speak their language or even admit where they're from.

But the masseuse was not one of those expatriates. She switched into Russian immediately.

"How long have you been here?" she asked.

She was not wondering how long I'd been leafing through *Vogue* in the waiting room.

"I was born here," I said.

"Your parents?"

"Born here, too."

Now that the initial assumption of my Russian-ness had broken down, things grew more complicated. She didn't know what to say.

"I'm not Russian," I explained. "I'm American. I learned Russian as a foreign language. I work as an interpreter and do written translations too." This explanation, while it made me exotic, placed us back on solid ground.

On that first visit, she peppered me with questions. Was I married? Yes. First time? No, second. What did my husband do? How old was I? Forty. So was she. Did I have children? She was a grandmother. I was childless.

I learned that she was an ethnic Russian from Kazakhstan, a vast former Soviet country I'd visited for my work a few times back in the nineties. She had a grown daughter who had remained behind. She mentioned an American husband. Then she sighed, commented on how different Americans and Russians are, and never referred to him again.

Months passed between appointments; as a freelancer, I indulged in such luxuries rarely. But when more coupons arrived in the mailbox, I set aside the one for the spa, and when I could, I booked an appointment with Helen. Her availability was always wide open; I rarely saw another client there. The place was beautifully appointed, with a large staff, all Russian-speaking, who were very professional when called upon to work but seemed to spend most of their time drinking tea. What really goes on at this establishment? I wondered.

Going there was like traveling to Russia for the afternoon. Helen would give a joyous cry of greeting, and then, although she had never met my parents, she would ask after them as if she had grown up next door. The electric samovar was always on the boil.

She lowered her voice one day and said, "If you come when the boss is away, I can give you a special price. Any procedure you want. Just don't tell the others." The last sentence was accompanied by a jerk of the head toward the other treatment rooms where her coworkers were presumably toiling. She tore a scrap of paper off the roll used to cover the massage table and wrote down her cell number. I dropped the scrap into my purse.

Once, while she was working on me, a coworker came in with a message. After the woman left, Helen whispered heatedly, "She's a snake! Always spying and informing the boss. Watch out for that one."

Another time, she ran her finger over the scar on my left side and asked about it.

"I have lung disease," I explained. "My left lung collapsed two years ago. That scar is where the surgeon went into reinflate it and take the sample for the biopsy."

"Oh—" she said, at a loss for words.

To cover the pause, I said, "That's why I can't have children." Immediately, I regretted raising the subject. But for some reason I continued. "My doctors say pregnancy would make the condition much worse."

The moments that followed were oppressive. The sound of my breathing filled the room.

"We might adopt," I added.

"Hmmm, adoption is risky," she said. "You don't know what you're getting. It's not yours." She kneaded my buttocks pensively.

I grunted.

She poured oil on my scar and rubbed it over and over, as if trying to erase it and make my skin new.

After a long moment, she said, "You should adopt from over there!" She used the vague and enveloping term that Russian speakers use for the area that was once called the Soviet Union, and before that, the Russian Empire. "It's perfect. You speak the language, you've lived there. Yes, that's what you should do. Not through official channels, of course—too much paperwork, too many bribes. Here's what you do," she went on, warming to her subject. "You find a Russian woman who's pregnant and doesn't want to keep the baby. You know plenty of people there, right?"

Lying face down on the massage table made it hard to answer. Not that I had much to say. I tried to nod and hoped she would recognize it from the back for what it was.

"So, you ask everybody you know over there if they know anyone who's pregnant and planning to get an abortion. Then, you offer her money—dollars, of course—to carry the baby to term and give it to you. If you can't find a pregnant woman, well, then you find someone and you pay her to get pregnant. That way, you might even get to choose the father." She chuckled. "You bring the woman over here to live with you until the baby's born, so you can make sure she eats well and doesn't drink or smoke. And she could do some light housework, say, up until the seventh month. Vacuuming, laundry . . ."

Her hands fluttered down to my thighs. Every other massage therapist I'd gone to had left bruises. That was why I kept coming back to Helen.

"But if she comes over here and stays with you, you must not, under any circumstances, let her go out alone," she went on. "She might meet someone who offers to support her or give her a job, and then she'll get the idea that she can make it here without you. No, no, no, don't let her out of your sight the whole time she's here. Then, just as soon as that baby pops out, back home she goes on the next plane."

She continued. "When the baby is born, you can have the hospital record the birth as if you were the real mother. I'm sure they would do it if you slip them some cash. Then you wouldn't even have to adopt officially. There would never be any record that someone else gave birth. The baby would be yours, free and clear."

I lay still on the table as she spun her scenario. Oddly, it barely aggravated my sorrow; the plan was too far-fetched. I only wished I could relish it and believe in it as much as she seemed to.

After a while, Helen fell silent. She threw herself into her work. Slowly, she rubbed the soles of my feet, toes, one after the other, instep, heel. I stretched, arched, then relaxed back onto the massage table.

───────

I close my eyes. I soar. The hour is late, past midnight, but the last rays of the setting sun still streak the sky. Leningrad (as it was still called when I was a student there) is so far north that for a couple of weeks in late June and early July the sun doesn't set completely, and just a few hours later, it rises again. Summer is one single sunny afternoon that stretches on and on.

After the long, dim winter, people grow giddy from that excess of brightness. Crowds of young people surge along the Neva River embankment in this strange mingling of dark and light that is neither night nor day. A pale young man with long hair strums a guitar and sings in high, sweet tones. On a deserted side street, a damaged trolley cable spits balls of sparks into the twilight. They tumble onto the battered asphalt, shatter, and are extinguished.

Next I'm in a pantry filled with glass jars glinting purple, orange, ruby, green, and brown: it is my first mother-in-law's stock of preserves. They will see the family through the winter. Beets, apricots, strawberries, green beans, and walnuts swim in sweet or savory juices. Prying the lid off one of those jars is a sacrament. The sound of the breaking seal promises indescribable gustatory delight. In an economy of scarcity, this bulging pantry is better than money under the mattress.

Now I'm standing on a cliff in the Caucasus Range in a small knot of people, holding hands with Aleksandr. We look down to where two rivers flow into each other, their green and brown waters swirling together like some strange cocktail, and then the two colors blend to form a new tint, which is both and neither. The new river rushes foaming down its course. All the wedding parties in this town make their way here to gaze down; it's local tradition.

I see other scenes too, these in America. I'm omitting a lot, almost everything, in fact; none of it belongs here, as I've already said. I've lived a long time now, and when I look back, there's too much. Many things must be skipped over: a dizzying courtship in a foreign land, life with the in-laws over there, coming back to America, trying to help him settle here, and arguments about having children—him: not yet; me: why not?—and other things, the marriage on life support, recognition of failure, division of our modest assets, signing of papers, parting of ways. Tears. More tears. I've replayed these scenes too often. I want to turn away.

———————

Helen slipped out of the room, leaving me to emerge from the dream state induced by her ministrations. I rose slowly and dressed, concealing my scars beneath layers of clothing.

As I settled the bill and thanked her, she said in the low voice that signaled intrigue, "I might be able to find a woman over there who's willing to give you a baby. My daughter might know someone. Would you like me to ask the next time I call her?"

"I'll talk to my husband first," I said, placing a large tip on the counter and pushing it toward her. It was not completely a lie. That evening, I knew, I would tell Tristan the story of Helen and we'd laugh. But the conversation would not be a discussion of whether we should acquire a child in the way she suggested.

"I'll let you know," I told her in parting.

Months later, I returned to the spa for the balm of her touch on my ragged shoulders.

"Have you thought about what I suggested?" she asked casually, unfolding a sheet for me to lie on. I climbed up, breathing hard. My condition had deteriorated since my last visit.

"Yes," I said into the table. "My husband doesn't think it's a good idea." That would certainly have been true had I presented it to him as a real possibility.

"Oh, well," she said. "Don't worry. Maybe it wasn't meant to be. Maybe you aren't destined to have children. Who needs children, anyway? They're nothing but headache and heartache. So, enjoy life!" She bit into the final phrase in a tone of mad gaiety.

"That's it, just enjoy life!" she repeated. She was practically shrieking.

She placed her hands on either side of my skull and rubbed the bones of my head with her thumbs, hard. The sound of my hair scraping against my scalp was terribly loud.

A few weeks later, I was riding back from my parents'. The driver had that accent. I wasn't going to say anything, I swear. Then he asked about the book in my hand. He said, "Do you like to read?" followed, God knows why, by, "Do you speak any other languages, or just English?"

I said yes. That was all. Then he wanted to know which ones. So I told him. And he was off. In Russian.

He came from Georgia, he said. He'd come to America as a boy in the seventies, when Jews were leaving the USSR in droves. His father had managed a factory in the Soviet Union and escaped the country one jump ahead of the KGB, having been tipped off that they were going to arrest him for some kind of fraud. It was impossible to manage a factory in the Soviet Union without running afoul of the law somehow. That was just how things were set up there.

So, his father bribed somebody to get permission to leave the country without delay and bribed someone else to get plane tickets for the family. Various people, including some members of the secret police, ended up spending years in prison because they were loyal friends and refused to inform on him. He sent out the family gems, icons, and art treasures to his brother, who owned a falafel restaurant in Tel Aviv. The plan was that the uncle would hold onto the goods until they reached America, then sell everything and wire them the money to start their new life.

The uncle kept everything. The driver and his parents never saw any of it. His father plucked chickens on an assembly line in Baltimore. Later he opened a dry-cleaning business, then a fast-food franchise, and after that, a home furnishings store, which grew into a chain.

His father and his uncle never spoke again. Two years ago, a cousin had written to say that the uncle had died of a heart attack while taking a mud bath at a sanatorium on the Dead Sea.

We were a block from my building when the driver said, "Are you a writer?"

I sighed. "Yes."

"Have you been published?"

"A little bit," I said. "In some magazines."

"Oh really? Which ones? Maybe I've seen your work!" he said excitedly.

"I don't think so."

"I want to write a book about my father and my uncle, but I've tried, and I don't think I can do it myself. I want the entire world to know what a bad person my uncle was. His daughter wrote a book about what a fine person he was, and it was all lies. Not a word about the icons and the jewels and paintings he stole. Do you think if I wrote a book it would be successful? Do you think someone might want to make a movie out of it? Would you help me write it?"

"Well," I said, "what's important about a book is not so much what happens in it, but how the writer tells it. It's hard to say, based on what you've told me, if it would be successful."

He was holding my credit card. He took the imprint with his little machine and handed the receipt back to me to sign. I returned his copy.

"Would you help me?" he persisted. "You're a writer."

"It's your story," I said, switching to English. "Only you can tell it."

I opened the door a crack, put one foot on the ground, and waited for my credit card.

Dark Green and Velvety, with a Dusting of Cat Fur

ONE WEEK AND THREE DAYS. That's how long my manuscript has been with the agent.

I came to the agent through a friend, who said that I should expect to hear back in six to seven weeks at the earliest. That, she explained, is about normal for agents.

"The best, sanest response to sending out a manuscript," she added, "is to start writing something else right away."

She's had two novels on the *New York Times* Best Seller list and is now at work on her third. And so, with her as my guide, here I am: back on the couch. Not the psychotherapeutic couch. Not the casting couch. The writing couch.

This massive couch is dark green and velvety, with a dusting of cat fur. It reminds me of the Gump, the magical flying machine in *The Marvelous Land of Oz*, a book I used to read and reread. The Gump was constructed from two identical purple sofas roped together, as I recall, with a deer's head attached at one end and a palm frond at the other. My couch doesn't fly, but it has taken me many places.

An inheritance from my mother's two older sisters paid for the couch. Their bequest also covered my extended stays in Paris to learn French and the hospital bills for emergency surgery when I was uninsured.

The reason that the couch became the writing couch is because my writing process now involves a great deal of sleeping. That emergency surgery revealed my chronic degenerative lung disease, which is so debilitating that I cannot write for more than an hour and a half without pausing for a nap. (In fact, half an hour of shut-eye intervened between the end of the previous paragraph and the beginning of this one.) And while I certainly could write at my desk and climb the ladder to the loft bed each time I need to rest, writing and resting in the same place is highly efficient. Taking breaks without getting up cuts out the distractions, increasing the likelihood that I will resume work immediately on waking.

The book I just sent out took four years to write, four years spread out across six years. Spread out across six years, because there were two years in the middle when I abandoned the manuscript, convinced that I would never return to it. Plus half a year (which I now include in the four productive years) when I was working on something I thought would not fit into the book but that eventually found its way in.

During those years on the writing couch, I learned that I must have certain items within arm's reach while writing, otherwise things will not go well. Before settling down to work, I make my way around the room, gathering what I need and depositing it all in a pile on the couch: ChapStick, Kleenex, flash drive, any notes or books I may need, and my landline and cell phones. (I don't answer the phone when I'm writing, but I like to see who's calling.) I place a glass of water on a small table next to the couch. In all seasons, I wear a pair of wool socks and cover myself with the gray afghan with red trim crocheted by my grandmother, dead these forty years. I open the computer and off I go: write, sleep, write, sleep, write. This is the ideal sequence: three stints of writing intercut with two of sleep. It adds up to some four or five hours of writing, spread out across six or seven hours total. This is how I spend my weekends.

As I become engrossed, I feel the benevolent spirits of my aunts hovering close by. They were avid readers, as is my mother, the youngest. My grandmother (the same one who crocheted the afghan) was mystified by this love of literature; when one of her daughters brought home some new title, she would say, "Another book? Don't you already have some?"

Many of my aunts' books found their way into my personal collection while they were alive. Even more came to me after they died. If I'm unsure of the provenance of a particular volume on my shelf, it's a safe bet that it belonged to one of the aunts. Some of my books simply could not have come from anywhere else.

They gave me Grace Paley's two story collections for my birthday when I turned fourteen, telling me proudly that they'd been friends with her way back when she was a very young wife and mother, living the events that would later be transmuted into the stories. The original City Lights edition of Allen Ginsberg's *Howl*, thin and small enough to slip into a pocket, came from my Aunt Bea. It embodied her excitement about whatever was new, hip, and rebellious in every era it was given to her to witness, even long after most people her age had put away childish things. She gave me Pablo Neruda's memoirs (he was a communist like her), and I raced through them during my first weeks of college, throwing off the yoke of required reading.

Aunt Esther was the custodian of hard-to-find translations of Yiddish writers and books on race; it was from her that I inherited a novel in two volumes called *The Yeshiva*, set in the Polish-Lithuanian village where my grandfather grew up, and from her that I borrowed *Manchild in the Promised Land* when I was in my teens. When she died well over a decade later, I had not yet returned it.

Aunt Bea wrote for the newspapers. Near the end of her life, she brought out boxes and boxes of clippings to show me what she'd done, and when she died, I became their keeper. She did an interview with Julia Child for the *Times* Arts and Leisure section that began, "For anyone who loves fine food, an invitation from Julia Child to drop by for lunch sometime is like Vladimir Horowitz inviting a classical music lover to drop by some afternoon while he runs through a few Beethoven sonatas."

She profiled poet Anne Sexton, who confessed that the sole reason that she did not leave her husband, a successful businessman, was that in a good year her poetry and plays brought in no more than two thousand dollars. This did not go into the article. Sexton let it slip (along with other secrets that my aunt refused to divulge) because Aunt Bea asked around, found out the poet's favorite brand of vodka (apparently everybody had one in those days), and brought a bottle to the interview.

Aunt Bea did a piece on Janis Joplin too. There was no heroin involved, as far as I know.

Waiting for an agent to respond; advice from a friend wise in the ways of the literary marketplace; the couch where I write and sleep and write; the aunts who posthumously bestowed the couch upon me; those aunts' personal libraries and writings—what unites the disparate items on this list?

I have finished a book, and for the first time in six years (minus two years of abandonment), I must begin again. Beginnings are cobbled from disparate things. Beginnings develop beyond themselves and grow into something more when links are forged between those disparate things. Writing a long work teaches you everything about writing, except how to start over. And over. The hard part of finishing is beginning again.

I check my email. No word from the agent. Five weeks and four days to go.

The screen swims before my eyes; I yawn ferociously. Time for another nap.

Infelicities
of Style

2.

LAST NIGHT, I DREAMED I saw Lloyd Geduldig. Dusk was falling. Alongside a grain silo just outside the town, his broad, pale face hovered low, like an early moon.

The silo stood near a T-junction, and just behind it, tread marks cut across a field. Clumps of mud were strewn about: a tractor had recently traveled the rut, tearing up the ground. Apart from that, all was thickly covered with snow.

Yes, the dream came complete with an old-fashioned winter, the kind we used to curse as we stamped our feet at the bus stop, the kind upstate New York has not seen these thirty years. And on the hillside, the bare trees were like pencil strokes. Just the way I remember.

I didn't care if my moving arm disturbed people in the nearby seats. If the sibilant scratch of pen speeding across paper or the occasional crackle of pages turning in my spiral notebook distracted others from the action onstage, I didn't care. I was busy pinning down my immediate, my strong reactions. I sensed obscurely that if I could capture those responses and also seize the reader with a powerful first sentence, good copy was within my grasp.

But as I took notes, writing at times with such vehemence that my pen dug into the page underneath and the page behind that,

I sometimes wondered: who would take my writing seriously if they knew who was behind the byline? I was a freshman at the local college, just seventeen years old. The years mount and mount; the question hovers.

As the applause died away, I would rush from the theater — the deadline for the morning paper fell at midnight — and make for my dorm room, settle in at the keyboard, and roll a blank sheet into the portable Olivetti, a gift from my mother when I left for college.

But computers were about to become the big thing. Nobody had their own machine yet; a company called Apple donated several rooms full of them to the school, and then I would go to one of those rooms after the performance to write the review and print it out. Sometimes, especially when term papers were coming due, there was a long wait. You got the computer for forty-five minutes; if you needed more time, you had to log off and put your name on the list again. And there were always more people in line: some reading, some writing, some bedded down on the floor, their heads pillowed on knapsacks filled with textbooks.

While I waited, I would make more scrawls in my notebook. When at last my name was called, I worked rapidly to weave my notes into something more substantial — substantial yet brief, for Lloyd had said to keep it to 750 words.

———

If I was lucky and got two free tickets, my boyfriend came too. While I wrote the review afterward, he sat patiently, headphones clamped to his ears, listening to his tapes for Japanese class.

When I finished, we descended the long cobbled hill from the campus into the sleeping town. We crossed the pedestrian mall with its darkened stores, then went one block further, down State Street, past the movie palace and the tobacco-store Indian. The door of the newspaper office had a drop slot for nocturnal submissions, down low, near the ground.

The deadline met, we continued for a few blocks more, almost to the far edge of the town, to the all-night diner by the railroad tracks. I usually ordered chili, washed down with a strawberry milkshake; the boyfriend always had a burger with fries and a Coke. We split the check, then trudged back up to the dorms. We rarely spent the night together; we both had roommates.

———————

I bolted awake early and ran out to buy the morning paper. I flipped through it, searching for my name, my words. I pulled out the extra copy of the typescript I'd kept from the night before and compared my draft with the published version, puzzling out the reasoning behind the edits.

A few days later, the mail would bring an envelope addressed in tiny, crabbed script. In the enclosed note on newspaper letterhead, the editor would comment on my work, signing with his initials, L. G. "Nice work, save a few infelicities of style," said a typical missive, following up on a piece of mine about a postmodern dance troupe from the great metropolis downstate that had passed through on a one-night stopover. The infelicities were gone.

The note always came wrapped around a check for twenty-five dollars. This was before direct deposit.

———————

My first meeting with Lloyd is one of the things I barely remember now. It probably followed a cold call, dorm room to newspaper office; I had a knack for cold calls back then; when I was seventeen, eighteen, twenty, twenty-five, the essentials—jobs, housing—were in constant flux. I was always chasing after some necessary thing.

Whoever picked up the phone at the *Journal* would hear that on the strength of a few years of ballet lessons and some library books about dance that I'd pored over until the pages wore thin beneath my gaze, I wanted to take over doing their dance reviews, and that person, having no idea what to tell me (on the phone, I sounded even younger than I was), must have passed me to Lloyd. I never found out what his job title was exactly, but he had authority. People got passed to Lloyd when nobody else knew what to do with them.

Here is the sum total of what I recall about Lloyd. He was already old when I knew him, at least forty-five. He wore suspenders and was rarely without a pipe. From time to time, he made a passing reference to his early life in Britain. His accent had been sanded down by long years in the United States, it seemed to me. Why he came to America, and whether he brought a family with him, left one behind, started one here, or some combination of the above — this I never learned.

Mainly what I knew about Lloyd was that as an editor he took infinite pains with his own work and that of others, perhaps not even distinguishing clearly between the two. He had the penmanship of someone whose attention to the crucial, minute detail caused him untold anguish.

And he was out of place in the bustle and rush of a newspaper office. Even at seventeen, I could tell that he was not meant to work in a newspaper office. He should have been up on the hill, at the college, teaching something. I had no idea why he was at the bottom instead of the top, only that the bottom was the wrong place.

———

How I recently found those articles that I wrote for him, after several afternoons spent sifting through the contents of my basement storage unit, and what else I came across in the course of the search — the class notes and assignments from elementary through graduate school; the drafts upon drafts of stories and essays, some published, many not; the letters of rejection, some professional, some personal; the diaries; and the masses of other logorrheic outpourings that constitute the dispiriting detritus of my past—all while continuously inhaling a peculiar dry mist that rose off these mounds of paper—that is a story for another time.

What matters is that I now hold in my hands the file containing those thirty-year-old rectangles of newsprint scotch-taped to onionskin, about fifteen of them, each one hand-labeled with its publication date and the words "the Journal." The file also contains Xerox copies of each article—dozens of copies, in some cases. Apparently, I believed that in the years to come, I would blanket the countryside with copies of these articles in order to snag ever more jobs and writing assignments. Whether this was a sign of youthful optimism (a belief in the power of my articles to convince editors and employers of my worth; dreams of a career marked by variety and movement) or pessimism (a belief that I would never improve on those articles, that I would be unable to find one thing and stick with it), I cannot say.

————————

One glance at the clippings, and the topographic map of that small slice of upstate New York shakes itself open in my mind once more: I see a long valley that is home to a deep, narrow lake extending for miles and ringed by low, tree-covered hills. At one end is the town of Ithaca. It starts on the valley floor, then climbs the nearest hill, where it becomes the university, then spills down over the back of the hill, spreading out gradually into shopping malls, filling stations, and farmland.

Slicing down across the hills all around the valley are deep, boulder-lined gashes in the earth. The water roars through them. Once you descend the trail into one of those gorges, the sole traces of human presence are the strong, graceful bridges that curve over the rushing water and the chains that hang across the footpaths barring entry, low enough to step over without strain.

Especially in winter, the town seems remote, isolated, although there are other towns around, even smaller ones. Many of the villages and towns and even the hamlets in that region bear antique names: Ithaca, Marcellus, Troy, Pompey, Homer, Utica, Syracuse, Cicero. The first white people to come here were raised on the glories of Greece and the grandeur of Rome, and the toponyms they affixed make the place seem remote in time, as well as space.

But pull back slightly from that imaginary map, and you see that just a few hours' drive southeast of the town sits one of the world's largest, liveliest cities, giving the lie to the notion that this place is far from everything. The artistic output thrown off by that frenzied metropolis, like sweat off a spinning dancer, regularly lands all the way up here.

———————

And so I covered whatever came to town, mostly from New York City: ensembles that poured electronic sound and video projections over their movement like piquant sauce over rancid meat; dancers moving in silence; dancers chosen precisely because they were untrained; choreography that looked like sauntering down the street backward; performers wearing shirts with numbers and symbols on them standing side by side to form equations; dance plus spoken word; dancers carrying signs; dancers in high heels; dancers in basketball shoes; dancers going barefoot; dancers wearing spandex; dancers wearing flapper dresses; dancers wearing nothing; obese dancers; anorexic dancers; dancers gaunt from a disease that few people back then had heard of; dances entitled *Three Dances*, *Evidence of Dancing*, *Punctuation*, *Array*, *Watershed*, *Encounter*, *Accompany*, *Rotary Motion*, *Continuous Replay*, *TV Reel*, *Smoke Signals*, *Rumble in the Jungle*, *Winter Green*, *Soft Broil*, and *Share the Wine and Bread That Is Our Blood-Ochre Love*.

And I struggled to make sense of dance that was probably meant *not* to make sense. Whoever wrote the headlines at the newspaper picked up on my bafflement. "Skillful much ado about nothing?" read the banner over one of my pieces. "Dance company mystifies with astringent simplicity," said another.

"Watching avant-garde dance is frustrating," I wrote of one performance, now long forgotten. "It supplies no answers. Its practitioners smash the same icons again and again and then hop about barefoot and gleeful on the smithereens." I referred to the "antitraditions of the postmodern—denial of spirit and of variety; bleak minimalism, choreographed facelessness."

"This is no-frills dance without a structural plan. Its random organization and lack of purpose doom all attempts at analysis. One learns to watch and tries not to wonder," I wrote one evening as midnight loomed.

———————

Then there was the local ballet troupe, a family affair; the matriarch provided the choreography and what artistic direction there was, while her three grown daughters performed the leads in an endless stream of *Nutcrackers*, *Cinderellas*, and *Pinocchios*, backed by prepubescent girls staggering about in toe shoes, their faces taut with pain and fear. Every performance illustrated the universal dilemma of the small-town ballet school: Should it issue the coveted satin footgear while the student dancers' bones were still soft and prone to injury, or wait until the girls were ready? This school had decided to hand them out early; if it did not, went the reasoning, the girls would go elsewhere to get their pink, beribboned slippers, to a dancing school where negligent teachers would start them out on pointe too vigorously, leading inevitably to strains and sprains.

"Someone must save the children of the Upstate Ballet," read my lede, after I had seen the little girls contorted on the very tips of their toes once too often.

"I can't run that," said Lloyd in a tone of gentle rebuke when we crossed paths the next afternoon at the ice-cream parlor downtown. "Community relations, you know."

My favorite performer, a woman with massive, muscular thighs and long blonde hair that slid in a curtain across her face, was not from New York or from the town. She lived in the town somewhere, or near it, but she was not of it. She was a refugee from South Africa, that's what I'd heard, had danced with a ballet troupe there, and because of some unspecified act that ran counter to apartheid—dancing on stage in the arms of a black man?—she had been forced to flee.

Now she was a sort of Isadora Duncan type, doing improvised solo shows. She performed without music, pausing in odd positions to make off-the-cuff remarks about the venue and the audience or her state of mind that evening and reciting what was apparently poetry, sometimes in a guttural language that may have been her native Afrikaans, sometimes in a very different-sounding language that, according to someone in Africana Studies at the college, was probably Zulu. Which supposedly she had learned during an abortive stint as the junior wife of a Zulu chief.

Her technique was powerful and impeccable. She moved as if in a trance, and because of the no-music rule (it was a distraction, she explained in one of her impromptu addresses), you could sometimes hear her joints popping. Dancing alone, barefoot and barelegged, in silence, without sets, in a black or gray t-shirt and skirt outfit so simple that you could hardly call it a costume—these things might have been limitations for some dancers, but the absence of trappings freed her to reach new heights.

She allowed no reviews and no photographs. I was permitted to attend under solemn oath not to write about her for the paper. Someone before me had broken a similar promise and been banned from her performances in perpetuity. In any case, there is no point in attempting to describe how she moved. Her movements were extremely simple. She was transcendent, and while we watched, we were too.

Dozens of men and women in the town were in love with her. A woman I knew slightly, Leah was her name, told me she'd hosted a performance at her art gallery, and afterward, thinking everyone had left, she'd gone into the storeroom in the back to switch off a light she didn't recall turning on in the first place, and there was the dancer, surrounded by a clutch of admirers. She was standing on a table with her arms raised, and people were on their knees, reaching toward her. The only sound, said Leah, was breathing.

The dancer never charged admission. No one knew for sure how she lived, or where. Word was that she'd been taken in by squatters on the fringes of town who were trying to make a go of an abandoned farm with an apple orchard.

The programs and locations of her performances were not announced; you found out by word of mouth. Her dances had no titles and were never repeated. She danced in small upstairs spaces above bars, and in private homes. I saw her perform in the lobby of a movie theater following the regular midnight screening of *The Rocky Horror Picture Show*, on a tiny stage in a converted doughnut factory, and at an abandoned gas station, embracing the pumps as if they were immobile partners in the dance.

Sometimes, owing to a last-minute change of venue, the audience piled into cars and drove somewhere in a convoy, and only the driver of the lead car knew where they were headed. Did she fear persecution here as well? Did it have something to do with her immigration status? Hidden beneath a blanket in the back of a pickup truck, she had come in over an unguarded sector of the border with Canada where it cuts across the Mohawk reservation. Because she feared deportation, no one knew her given name. She was known as Spinningwing Wheatgrass (not her real alias) — two words, capital S, capital W. She always emphasized that when introducing herself, though nobody had any reason to write it down. Not three words, and not four, she would say, but two.

Writing arises from loss; it aims to fashion something to fill the charred void that is one of the late phases of suffering, to erect on a parched plot of pain an edifice of meaning, or of beauty. I made myself into a teenaged dance reviewer when I failed as a dancer.

In high school, back in Syracuse, I was an indifferent, once-a-week ballet pupil, until the director of the ballet school, a tiny, fierce woman named Gunilla, placed a fateful phone call to my mother. Gunilla, who had performed with the Royal Ballet of Lapland before marrying an American and washing up in central New York, told my mother I had promise. I should take ballet classes more often, she said — every day, in fact — if I wanted to dance "seriously."

My mother reported the conversation, and my future opened out before me in an instant: I was meant to be an artist.

Contemplating this, I wheeled my bike out of the garage. I flew down hills, poised on one pedal, a leg extended behind me in arabesque, back arched, head raised. My hair streamed out behind me. I switched legs every block or so. Coasting, I imagined my life as a dancer.

Gunilla was a shrewd businesswoman. She made no explicit promises or predictions, did not say I actually had what it took to make it as a professional dancer; she let me fill in the blanks. And so, from my twelfth through my sixteenth year, I went to the ballet school six days a week. Probably enrollment was down and she needed the income.

Very soon, I began to suspect that I was no prima ballerina assoluta in the making. I was too old to develop the necessary technique, too weak, too graceless. I lacked flexibility. I was no sylph, either — and even that would not have been enough, for what professional ballet demanded of women and girls back in the seventies was anorexia, nothing less.

But I had tasted devotion to a calling, and I did not want to give that up, stand down, accept that I was not among the chosen. For those four years, I soldiered on. It was not a waste of time.

I read about ballet, and through its prism I learned something of European history, art, and music. I discovered the Romantic era and the Russian Revolution. I picked up dozens of French words and a handful of Russian ones. The names Delibes, Petipa, Fokine, Diaghileff, Théophile Gautier, Chopin, Aaron Copeland, and Stravinsky came to mean something.

I learned that during the Romantic era, rival ballerinas at the Paris Opera would put ground glass in each others' ballet slippers, and that dancers' costumes sometimes caught fire from the gaslights that illuminated the stage in those days; that when asked how he achieved his spectacular jumps, Nijinsky explained that he went up in the air, stayed there a while, and then came down; and that during Balanchine's early hardship years in America, he choreographed for circus elephants.

I obtained a bilingual edition of Mallarmé's collected poems and read "Afternoon of a Faun," my eyes gliding from the French side to the English and back again. That led, by an intricate series of moves I can no longer reconstruct, to William Butler Yeats, Edna St. Vincent Millay, T. S. Eliot, Baudelaire, and Rimbaud. I learned that all artistic practice, no matter the genre or the form, requires a certain level of technical mastery, where, as I knew, I fell far short, and that to achieve greatness, something beyond technique was required, something transcendent, something wild.

The story has a happy ending. I was saved from years of futile striving by a diagnosis of shin splints. Shin splints consist of many minute fractures in the long bone below the knee; frequent jumping widens the fractures and prevents healing.

The doctor prescribed seven months of no ballet. He handed the sentence down lightly; he knew nothing of my ambitions and what this would do to them. (My dance teachers said that after such a long hiatus I would never recover such technique as I had.) I did not tell him and did not bargain for a lighter sentence.

At subsequent appointments, he studied my X-rays and extended the ban for more months. Still, I said nothing. Some part of me welcomed this way out. It saved me from acknowledging that I was giving up because I just wasn't good enough.

For many months, I mourned the loss.

———————

A few weeks into my new life of no dancing, I sat, along with all the teachers and most of the students, in the hallway of my old ballet school—I still thought of it as mine. (Gunilla was no longer with us; no one knew exactly where she was. Her name had been linked for some time with that of a wealthy local balletomane, then she'd had a baby whose paternity was the subject of intense speculation, followed by a divorce from the man who'd brought her to upstate New York. Finally, she'd filed for bankruptcy and stopped showing up at the school. After that, the trail goes cold.)

Tense excitement hovered. A small man appeared at the far end of the hall, swathed in a gray wool overcoat and tinted wrap-around glasses. He walked rapidly in our direction. We all held our breath as we watched his approach. No one said it, no one needed to say it: we all believed, our teachers too, that seeing how this man walked down the hallway, every step he took, would teach us something priceless that we could learn in no other way. And he was right here, at our school.

American Ballet Theatre was in town, giving nine performances in one week, and Lillian, the school's new director, had offered her studio as a rehearsal space. It was close to the theater, she reasoned, and no worse equipped than any of the other local plié parlors. The administrator who accepted the offer on behalf of ABT informed her that while a rehearsal or two might be open to a small number of advanced dance students, most would take place behind closed doors. The company members required utter privacy, she explained, in order to work with new partners and concentrate on unfamiliar or difficult roles.

Although the little ballet school was caught in a ceaseless struggle for survival, there was never any suggestion that the internationally renowned troupe might pay for its use of the premises. But, like Gunilla before her, Lillian was a shrewd businesswoman. She recognized a win-win situation when she saw one. Glimpsing ballerinas hurrying down the hall to the studio for their closed rehearsal would provide mysterious benefits for the student dancers; sharing the dressing room, even if the students were too awestruck and the visiting stars too preoccupied to exchange any words, would sprinkle us with enchantment. And maybe, just maybe, when word got out about the celebrities frequenting our school, enrollment would soar.

The man in the wool coat passed us without a glance and disappeared into the dance studio.

We stayed put, though we knew he would probably not reemerge for hours. But the door opened unexpectedly soon. The wraparound glasses and the wool coat were gone. In a unitard and ballet slippers now, the small man peered out, and in a thick accent we knew to be Russian only because we'd heard that he was from Russia, he asked for water. Then he closed the door.

Gesturing to us to stay put, Lillian jumped up and filled a mug at the same rusty drinking fountain where the ballet students lined up to gorge on ice-cold water after every class. She knocked at the door of her studio. It opened slightly. The man reached out, took the mug and drained it, handed it back, and again shut the door.

Lillian would never wash that mug again. On a yellow index card, she would write: Mikhail Baryshnikov, March 19, 1981, and tape it to the handle. The mug would occupy the place of honor on her desk and would not move from the spot until she left for California with an older ballet student who had never been quite right after he came back from Vietnam, and they became live-in caretakers at an upscale residential development in Marin County.

———

During that week when Baryshnikov drank our fountain water from Lillian's mug and his reflection came and went in our mirrors, we were permitted into our studio long enough to see tiny Natalia Makarova warming up at the barre, right heel on left shoulder, knee folded in back of her head, and Olympian Cynthia Gregory working on her pirouettes.

Gregory was having a bad day: she kept falling sideways off her pointes. Then she nailed it. She windmilled around four, five, six times. The other dancers stopped their warmups and gazed as her head and shoulders swung round and round, bringing the rest of her superbly tall body with them. As her spinning slowed, someone in the back emitted a low, protracted whistle. She came down from her pointes, jutted a hip forward in a jazzy fourth position, and grinned as her colleagues' applause broke over her.

———

Someone who has moved an ocean away, someone who didn't write back, someone who has fallen out of touch despite all the new devices designed to make that impossible, said to me once that if we consider wasted the hours and days we've spent with people we no longer see, then a very great part of our lives would be wasted indeed. Even as people disappear from our lives one by one, like tiny lights blinking out, those hours and days retain their value, for we have lived them.

Surely the same holds for the hours and days spent, in decades past, attempting to master an art form.

Just a few weeks before American Ballet Theatre came to town, before the orthopedist barred me from ballet, I might have deluded myself briefly, despite my underlying awareness that I was not meant to be a dancer, that someday that might be me with my right foot on my left shoulder, that might be me stopping my fellow dancers in their tracks with my quintuple and sextuple pirouettes.

Now I knew that would never be me.

About a year later, I volunteered to usher when the New York City Ballet had its turn in our town. The head usher, pockmarked, with a limp and a speech defect, commented familiarly on the dancers' performances, referred to the principals by first name and called the artistic director "Mr. B.," as the dancers themselves were said to do. (The more ardent balletomanes among us knew this tidbit from the press.) All this despite a paucity of evidence that she had ever exchanged a word with any of them.

In exchange for doing everything she said, which mainly meant donning the scratchy brown polyester vest that was our uniform and using a small flashlight to guide ticket holders to their places, ushers were granted free admission to all nine performances and the right, once the house lights dimmed, to drop into any unoccupied seat.

One evening when I did so, there, before a luminous blue scrim, was the fabled Suzanne Farrell being manhandled by Peter Martins. Or so it appeared from my seat in the orchestra; not every dance is made to be viewed from the expensive seats.

Holding her firmly by the wrists, Martins pushed Farrell away, then pulled her back, then lifted her over his head with one hand and, lowering her, gripped her thighs with such force that dimples formed in her nearly nonexistent flesh. They were both dressed in white. Indigo light washed over them. They panted furiously. In raspy whispers, they counted beats and murmured, "Okay—ready—go!"

As Martins put Farrell through her paces, his hands sliding rapidly over the stiff material of her bodice, their sweat showered down on me in the second row. Drops clung to my hair and rolled, burning, into my eyes. Drops coursed in rivulets down my cheeks.

———————

This story is unfolding in reverse. It starts near the end, then backs up a few decades, then chugs back another few years, kind of like that avant-garde choreography out of New York City that looked like sauntering backward down the street. My years in the southeast corner of the state—I always knew I'd end up a New Yorker, and here I am—are leaving their mark; my writing like the work of some choreographer experimenting in a downtown loft in the eighties, back when rents were low.

If he were my editor still, Lloyd would no doubt untangle the strands of this piece and place everything in order. Or not—perhaps he would see some merit in it and let it stand. He was the rare editor who could let things stand. And when he didn't, you were grateful to him for saving you.

But whatever he might have done with these pages, it is time now to return to the ending, which is where I began.

In our final conversation, Lloyd apologized that a review of mine had gone to press a day late. He'd mislaid it on his desk.

"I'm somewhat distracted," he said in a voice turned husky. "It's because I just separated from my wife, you see."

We had traveled much too far in a single sentence. I was suddenly beyond my depth. Twenty-one by then, I knew nothing of marriage or marriages and even less about how they end, sometimes. I could not fathom the suffering that this news carried, and I did not see that notwithstanding the monstrous cargo of pain in his words, his characteristic elegant restraint was, in fact, still in place. Any anxiety I felt on that score was misplaced.

He would not have permitted himself an infelicity, especially not then; I failed to give him the credit he deserved. My justification: at the time, I was constantly dodging laughable invitations from men who were way, way too old.

I mumbled something about studying for a final and got off the phone. I graduated and went far away.

———————

And then there he was, in my dream. I had barely recalled him in twenty-five years, did not know where he was, googled. Up came his obituary, floating across the cyber sky like words trailing behind a zeppelin.

He had died in a hospital, aged seventy-five, of an unnamed illness. The obituary was silent on his British connection. Cleveland-born, it said, he was survived by a son in Ohio; loved animals and opera; had received a master's degree in classics.

He had held teaching posts in ancient Greek and Latin at two colleges before becoming a newspaper editor. The colleges' names were given; one was on the hill just opposite my alma mater. Aha, I thought, and wondered what wrong turn his teaching career had taken. According to the obituary, he had come to the newspaper in 1981, which was just one year before he took my cold call.

His red suspenders and the pipe clenched between his teeth, often unlit, made it into the obituary as well. Also, a woman described as his long-time partner. His coworkers loved him, it said; he liked to stalk about the editorial office playing the curmudgeon, although he was in fact the soul of kindness; and death had come while he was in the midst of writing an authorized history of the local opera company. In his younger years, he had parachuted from a plane ninety-nine times, for sport.

The obituary answered some questions and left others forever open. One outstanding mystery is why he kindly took me on, so young, to do something clearly beyond my capacities, providing only the guidance I needed, and perhaps a bit less, so as to stretch me. His teaching and his exile from teaching (for I hold it as certain that he wanted to continue and that something interfered, something academic, something political, something small) — perhaps these experiences enabled him to teach people, wherever he found them, whatever it was they needed to learn.

Why is this girl writing about dancing instead of dancing?

Why is this man at the city desk instead of behind a lectern?

To give voice to these questions would have been infelicitous. What we do wherever we end up, that's the important thing; I believe that this was Lloyd's conclusion.

Losing
the Nobel

𝒩

I'D BEEN EARNING my living as a Russian-English interpreter for a decade and a half when I was hired to give English voice to one Svetlana Alexievich, an author slated to appear at the 2005 PEN World Voices Festival in New York City, where I live. I'd never heard of her; back then, few in the West had.

I learned as I prepared for the assignment that she was a former newspaperwoman whose books were based on interviews she did with plain Soviet and post-Soviet folk about their experiences of calamities such as World War II and the Soviet war in Afghanistan. Most recently, she had traveled to Chernobyl, borne witness to the consequences of the nuclear disaster, and then reported back, conveying in the locals' own words their grotesque sufferings and also those of the first responders, ordinary firemen sent into the fray in their shirtsleeves, absolutely innocent of radiation safety training or expertise.

The Russian language lacks a term for oral history, and so, with refreshing disregard for the sometimes heavily fortified border separating fiction from nonfiction, Alexievich had come up with her own, calling her books "novels in voices," or simply "novels." This despite the fact that their content came verbatim from taped interviews, had no narrative through-line, and swapped in a new protagonist every couple of pages. In addition to my day job with the Russian language, I was also trying to make a mark as a writer. Having toiled obscurely and intermittently for years in a difficult-to-name genre containing generous helpings of the lived, the observed, and the overheard, I instantly appreciated her confident blurring of distinctions that had long struck me as artificial and unnecessary.

Svetlana came from Minsk, the capital of Belarus, one of those new nations then poking up through the rubble of the Soviet Union. Her country was widely known as the last dictatorship in Europe. When I met her, she was persona non grata back home, having disgruntled the authorities somehow. She'd been living out of a suitcase for years, bouncing from one Western European capital to another, getting by on grants and gifts.

She was a small, sixtyish woman, shy, unpretentious. Her manner of speaking was urgent and heartfelt.

"For days after the blast at Chernobyl," she said at the festival, and I interpreted, "the bees stayed inside their hives. The worms burrowed a meter down into the ground. Those little creatures knew what to do. But what about us? What did we humans do? As always, we watched TV; we listened to Gorbachev; we played soccer."

Speaking of her genre and how she came to it, she said, "For us Slavs, talk is paramount. Life's mysteries are what we discuss. What is the essence, the core? As I sought my literary form, I came increasingly to understand that what I heard in the crowd was far more powerful than anything I was reading, and more affecting than anything that might flow from the pen of a solitary writer. Nowadays, one single person cannot write the all-encompassing book, as Dostoyevsky and Tolstoy used to do. The world has grown far too complex. But within each of us there lies a text: maybe two sentences, maybe half a page, maybe five pages, and these could be compiled into a joint opus. I realized that my books were in fact lying scattered about on the ground. I had only to pick them up."

Channeling her simple eloquence, I felt both euphoria and melancholy. My peculiar, fleeting intimacy with this remarkable woman and the interior of her mind seemed to place me on the cusp of something marvelous. Yet this sense that the best was yet to come was usually an illusion—I knew this. The climax was here; it was now.

She finished speaking; an instant later, I finished, and the main event was done. Over cheese cubes and wine in plastic cups in a rapidly emptying room, a few audience members praised my work effusively. For one moment, I thought that this heady praise was the very miracle I'd felt coming on.

Then I caught the number three train uptown. Full stop.

Except that Svetlana then passed my name to her agent, who passed it to a boutique publisher in the Midwest, who, some time later, approached me to translate two of her books into English.

––––––––––

I'd been a Russianist practically forever. I'd laid the groundwork in college, studying conversation, grammar, and literature, later honing my knowledge through total immersion behind the Iron Curtain, reading, movies, and, most important, long, long talks with native speakers from all walks of life. I'd translated books; I'd interpreted for statesmen and scoundrels, who were not infrequently one and the same; I'd devoted my working life to this language. You would think that my relationship with Russian, its writers, and its literature would be one of uncomplicated affection and intimacy.

But no. By my late thirties, my ties to Russian language and culture were growing increasingly tenuous. I had left my Russian-speaking husband years before. I had not set foot in Russia or its satellites in nearly a decade and had no plans to return. (As it turned out, I would go to Lithuania a few years later, but I didn't know that then, and that trip was unrelated to my work as a Russianist.)

I still spoke very fluently, however, for my immersion, dating to my twenties and early thirties, had been deep. Through the medium of Russian I'd learned crucial, cruel truths. In Russian I had fallen in love, and out. Despite my foreign accent and lapses grammatical, lexical, and cultural, Russian had in this way become almost native to me, as a close friend may become family, absent any tie of blood or marriage.

But that lingering fluency notwithstanding, I was now drawing down credit accumulated years before. Like some exiled Russian countess selling off the last of the emeralds and pearls sewn decades earlier into the hems and seams of her underthings, I was living off diminishing reserves, doing little apart from my daily work to replenish my storehouse of knowledge.

My initial reason for learning the language had been to read Russian literature in the original. Since freshman year in college, in response to the oft-repeated question, why Russian? I'd invariably replied that, having read *Anna Karenina* in English at age fourteen, my aim was to take her on in the original, vaulting clear over the heads of Constance Garnett, David Magarshack, and the rest of the literary translator pack.

But somehow, learning Russian had distanced me from Russian literature. It no longer made any sense for me to read the Russians in translation. Learning Russian had been painful— imagine your brain taken apart like a wristwatch, then reassembled, with a few parts left over that no longer fit anywhere. Choosing a translation over the original would strip those sufferings of all meaning. However, approaching Russian literature in the original was still daunting. And so, having devoted years to learning Russian, I now found myself in a limbo nearly devoid of Russian literature. It was as if I had scaled Mount Everest and was failing to take in the view—except during rare bursts, when, somehow mustering the strength to ignore my anxieties, I would binge-read in Russian for a few weeks. In this way, I fell in love with Pushkin, Chekhov, and Tolstoy, and, with time, built up the stamina to traverse vast tracts of Dostoyevsky.

But it took me years and years—well over a decade after I finished college—to make time for the unmediated *Anna*, and by then, it was not the same book I'd read at fourteen. No longer was it the story of a fetching woman, the flush of new love rendering her more fetching still, as she mazurkaed in the arms of a dashing suitor at an elegant ball. Now it was about that same woman's corpse laid out for identification in a railway shed, a cold sneer on her stiffening features; it was about men volunteering headlong for the Serbian-Ottoman War in order to flee their disastrous personal lives. This change was not, I think, due to the chasm that sometimes yawns between original and translation.

And of my total reading, Russian literature remained a very, very small part. There were great swaths of it that, at this rate, I would never know. During my years spent among the Russians, I had grown used to hearing people say things like, "Last year, I reread all of Russian literature," and this was actually conceivable, for, as Nabokov says early on in *Lectures on Russian Literature* (written, of course, in exquisite English), "the beautifully commodious thing about Russian prose is that it is all contained in the amphora of one round century—with an additional little cream jug provided for whatever surplus may have accumulated since."

But it was still too much for me.

The festival people sent a book of Svetlana's my way to help me prepare, an English translation called *Voices from Chernobyl*. The festival was coming up too quickly for me to lay my hands on the original, so I broke my no-translation rule.

A few pages in, I was jarringly reminded that reading translations from a language you know can be downright annoying. The errors are plain to see, even without the original close at hand. And a decade later, one mistranslation in that book haunts me still. Some of the first responders, away from home for months, frequented a brothel near the reactor. According to the translation, the "girls" from the brothel willingly *went for walks* with them, even though the men had been irradiated through and through.

Now, the Russian word *gulyat'*, "to take a walk," has a second, more colloquial meaning, vague yet suggestive, covering acts that range from promiscuous to debauched, and including sprees, binges, and escapades of all kinds. Clearly, the girls from the brothel had gone for much more than walks with the doomed emergency workers, but this was lost on the translator; Russian-born, he had left behind the land of his birth and his first language at age six, too young of course to grasp such meanings. His Russian had suffered a clear case of arrested development.

Nor, it was clear, had the publisher provided much oversight. Translation deeply affects a reader's relationship to any book originally written in a language she doesn't know, yet the boutique house responsible for *Voices from Chernobyl* apparently felt that such concerns hardly warranted much effort or expense.

No matter: the book gave me a general sense of Svetlana's work, which was what I needed to do the job.

———

I was in the middle of my life when the festival people started calling me to work with Russian-speaking authors—Svetlana was not the only one—and my life was falling apart. This was just after I'd been diagnosed with the degenerative, sometimes fatal pulmonary condition. Twice I had been hospitalized with a collapsed lung, and I was in evaluation for a double lung transplant. I had begun sleeping with an oxygen tube in my nose and was so short of breath that I could barely climb a flight of stairs or walk up a gentle slope.

In the face of serious malady, everything crumbles. Simultaneous interpreting being nearly as much about lung power as about language, I was increasingly unable to work. My debts were mounting. My health insurance coverage, which had over the years run the gamut from skimpy to nil, was tilting once again toward nonexistent.

Despite the coughing, weakness, and shortness of breath that were now a regular part of my days, I believed I could still do the festival gigs, which involved standing before large audiences alongside authors who represented the cream of contemporary Russian literature and instantaneously putting their utterances into English. And do them I could—if I spent the day in bed both before and after, and drove myself mercilessly the day of— for they lasted only an hour or so. When the author paused in thought, I sneaked a deep, deep breath and let it out, puff by puff: invisible smoke rings made from air.

And so, for years after I had to decline all other offers of inter- preting work, I continued to accept the festival gigs. They were a narrow bridge between my career as an interpreter, which was slipping from my grasp, and recognition as a writer, which I might never attain. For, on top of everything else, I was forty years old and had published not one single book of my own, only trans- lations of other people's books. The festival gigs allowed me to hold forth about writing before a rapt crowd, even if the words I uttered were not my own, even if the admiration I basked in was not meant for me.

Plus, they brought in some needed extra cash.

———————

Svetlana stayed in touch. Following the festival, she mailed a postcard from Paris and soon after that, a copy of *Boys in Zinc*, her book on the Soviet war in Afghanistan. On the flyleaf, she thanked me for my work at the festival, spoke of collaborations to come, and urged me to be happy, *in spite of everything*. A decade later, this untranslatably Slavic phrase remains mysterious to me.

I do not remember now if Svetlana in fact knew that I had translated books before, or if she innocently assumed that my ability to translate her spoken words meant that I would also be able to put her written words into English. Although the words "interpreter" and "translator" have become hopelessly confounded in the popular imagination, the work of the interpreter, who renders speech in one language into speech in another before a live audience or for broadcast, is in fact a far cry from that of the translator, who carries the written word over from one language into another while seated alone at her desk. One is not more difficult than the other; they are simply difficult in different ways.

I had tried for years to make my way in the world of literary translation but had repeatedly gotten sidetracked into translating other things—works of history; monographs on archaeology and philosophy; proposals to address needle-sharing in Kazakhstan, prostitution in Uzbekistan, the resurgence of polygamy in Tajikistan; phone tap transcripts of New York–based Russian organized crime suspects. ("How great to be in America and know we're not being bugged!")

I had gravitated toward literary translation in part because I hoped it could provide some writerly gratification, minus the risk of failure that shadows every attempt at translating the world into words. As I imagined it, I would spend engrossing hours sculpting sentences, and my name would appear on a title page, perhaps even a cover, but with none of the angst that comes of waiting, waiting for the next word to emerge from the void.

However, despite a few modest translation publications and a prize or two, it was not really working out. The good books and the interesting writers were going to other translators.

———

In the time before Svetlana, an eminent literary translator once got my number from somewhere and called in a panic. Her computer had swallowed ten chapters of a major glasnost-era novel that she was putting into English; the publisher was breathing down her neck; could I translate the missing piece, and could I do it right away? But I must not tell a soul, for the author, a dear friend of hers, would be terribly wounded if he learned that she'd farmed out a chunk of his masterpiece.

I knew this book as well as it is possible to know a work you've never read. My excuse, this time, was that the great poet Joseph Brodsky had famously dismissed it as *makulatura*, which literally means "old newspaper" or other dated paper goods fit only for the recycling bin, but can also mean something approximating "pulp fiction," only a whole lot less racy. It was about a band of Stalin-era university students, once close friends, later flung apart by history, with some rising to positions of power and deciding fates, while others were dispatched to the gulag.

When the book came out to great fanfare in 1987, I'd picked up a dozen copies at the hard-currency store in Moscow and, barely glancing at it myself, handed them out to Russians I knew. For, while it had not come under the censor's axe (if there still *was* a censor; this was one of those recurring murky periods in Russian history when no one quite knew what was going on), neither, for obscure reasons having to do with the vagaries of Soviet supply and demand, was it commercially available to ordinary Russians. It was such a hot ticket in Moscow that season that one day, upon returning to my hotel room unexpectedly in the middle of the afternoon, I walked in on three chambermaids sprawled across my bed, their frilly little aprons all askew, feather dusters forgotten on the floor, each one leafing through a copy of the book from the pile on the nightstand.

Now I agreed to translate lost chapters 23 through 32, encouraged by hints that this might lead eventually to other work that I could openly claim as my own. The deadline was so tight that I worked from a sheaf of xeroxed pages without seeing the rest of the book, for those chapters were the only ones provided, and I had given away my last copy years before. The respected literary translator massaged my bit to achieve a stylistically seamless fit with hers (and perhaps, it now occurs to me, with those of other subcontractors as well). She paid promptly, and when the translation came out, it landed in my mailbox, her name emblazoned across the cover beneath the author's, in a slightly smaller font. As expected.

After that, there was not another word from her, ever.

―――――――――

Eventually I would conclude, after hearing other translators' stories, that the best way to become a translator of contemporary literature is *not* to do uncredited work on behalf of a translator with a big name and few scruples, but rather to fall in with a bohemian crowd when you're in your twenties, sojourning in some foreign land and soaking up your chosen language.

You start translating as an act of friendship. One obscure, struggling novelist who drives a cab passes you on to another who works as a night watchman, who refers you to an unemployed poet who lives with his mother, and on and on. And if your bohemian pals form a rock band and you get roped in as the drummer or the lead singer, why, all the better, even if the group splits up after just a gig or two, for the shared experience would forge a close bond.

There are people who do this sort of thing and go on to translate entire schools or generations of contemporary authors in obscure Balkan or Slavic countries, some eventually settling and starting families there. You have to keep at it for years, though, doing without remuneration stuff that two or three decades on will make for delightful tales of a madcap youth, until your bohemian friends (well, a few of them, anyway) mature into acclaimed authors, sweeping you along with them, and you all become overnight sensations.

But what if you choose the wrong bohemian crowd? What if their creative strivings come to naught? God knows, it happens every day. We stride backward into the unfurling of time, blind to whatever is bearing down, and so such decisions must always be entirely uncalculating.

About a year after I worked with Svetlana at the festival, I landed the job in East Midtown, translating diplomatic correspondence and reports from Russian and French into English. (In a gamble that paid off, I charged the expenses associated with learning French for the job, including the stays in Paris and Montreal, settling the bill after I was hired.)

Passing a door left ajar, I would sometimes glimpse a senior colleague, hunched and Gogolian from decades in the international civil service, brandishing a crumbling typescript entitled *Instructions for Translators* and railing at some cringing junior translator about their errors: incorrect initial capitalization of treaty names, say, or a stray reference to "England" instead of "the United Kingdom of Great Britain and Northern Ireland" or failure to follow the house rule of inserting the standard closing for diplomatic correspondence ("Accept, Sir/Madame, the renewed assurances of my highest consideration"), regardless of what sentiment the original might express.

Sometimes I *was* that junior translator behind the door. Having worked independently nearly forever, I was unaccustomed to such treatment and did not accept it with good grace. But the job paid more handsomely than anything else I'd ever done or might hope to do.

Plus, it came with health insurance.

As I was settling into regular employment, the boutique Midwestern publisher sent along some pages from two of Svetlana's books that were as yet untranslated. Naturally, they wanted to see my work before signing a contract for the translation, and I, too, needed to know if I could inhabit the books daily, intimately, contentedly, for the years the work would take to complete.

On a night soon after the pages arrived, I struggled up the

stairs from the subway, stopping as usual at the top to pant a while, then made my way slowly home through the wintry dusk, pausing frequently to force the air in and out of my cold-stiffened lungs. After dinner, I sat down at the computer to tackle a section about Soviet women who had seen combat in World War II.

I was immediately transported to the front lines.

A nurse dragged two wounded soldiers from the battlefield, bullets whizzing overhead in the pitch-black night. She moved one of them toward the infirmary tent, set him down, and returned for the other. When the moon emerged from behind a cloud, she saw that one of the men wore a German uniform. She hauled him to safety nonetheless, and bound up his wounds.

"We tended to the enemy wounded, we Soviets did," she told Svetlana with modest pride.

A man recalled his role in the Soviet occupation of Germany late in the war. "Sometimes, there would be ten of us servicemen to one German girl," he said. "Ten men, one girl," he repeated in disbelief. "I was a good boy, from a cultivated family. To this day, I do not understand: How could I do this?" He paused. "We never, ever spoke to the girls in our unit about what we did. Oh, no. They were our comrades."

A young woman returned home when the fighting was over. At dawn, while everyone else in the house still slept, her mother shook her awake.

"The whole town knows where you've been," said the mother. "People have heard what you soldier girls got up to in the trenches with the men there. How will your little sisters find husbands if you stay here with us?"

She thrust a bundle at her and a heel of bread wrapped in newspaper.

"Daughter of mine," she said, "you must leave and never come back. Now, go."

I lavished hours on these brief passages. The words were simple; my dictionaries lay unopened. But each section had its own voice; every few pages, there was a new speaker, with a new idiolect. Each little segment had to sound exactly right.

As I translated, I pondered the changed contours of my days. Everything that mattered—my own writing, which I'd begun to approach with greater seriousness; the myriad details of managing a chronic illness, in itself a second job—had to be crammed now into a few hours a week. In the old, carefree (and nearly penniless) freelance days, I could have translated Svetlana by daylight. Now she too must be relegated to after hours.

I finished the pages and set them aside. Returning to them a few days later, I was dismayed: What had I done to Svetlana? Everything in my rendering was correct, yet none of it was right.

It struck me anew how ill-matched Russian and English are. So many Russian sentences lack an identifiable grammatical subject. Who is performing the action? This makes perfect sense in the Russian-speaking world, where impersonal forces have held sway since time out of mind, deciding fates and disposing with impunity of small and impotent beings.

In English, this leads to incomprehensible gaps. Yet if the subject was left implicit in the original, who was I to put a name to it in the translation? In Russian, everyone understood who was doing what. Hints were rife; unspecified connections were mysteriously clear. But what read as compelling and merely elliptical in Russian became, in English, a loose bundle of irrelevancies and non sequiturs. In Russian, there was a deep, narrow well of unuttered meaning in that small white space between the full stop at the end of one sentence and the uppercase letter that began the next. I might tumble into one of those wells, never to reemerge.

I declined the project, pleading health problems.

The years were whipping past; now I was in my late forties. At the job, the pay mounted and the miseries diminished, though at first these shifts were slow, verging on imperceptible. Financial security took hold. The lung disease, degenerative, slowed its advance, thanks to a wildly expensive little pill now covered by insurance. This pill, yellow, triangular, and puffy, like a tiny, magical sofa cushion, kept me off the transplant list, and maybe even — for who can say what might have been? — off the obituary page.

This newfound stability enabled me to spend hours each week putting my own words to paper and to send out my work (first-person stories, taken more or less directly from life) for publication. My own work — not translations, but originals — began appearing regularly in respected literary magazines. Although I expected every publication to be my last and was certain that my success as a writer would always be exceedingly modest, setting aside literary translation for writing seemed to me the only possible choice.

From time to time, my thoughts turned to Svetlana and to that opportunity I'd passed up. I imagined that the publisher must eventually have found someone else to translate the books. No doubt they were out there somewhere, in English, seeking their readers.

And then, nearly a decade after I had declined to translate them, I discovered that those books of Svetlana's, which I'd come to think of in some way as mine, were *still* unavailable in English, and that despite that fact, the London bookmakers had for several years been placing odds on her for the Nobel Prize in Literature.

A Nobel for oral history? It seemed unlikely.

According to the press reports, when Stockholm called, Alexievich was in the kitchen, doing her ironing. She said she'd use the prize money to buy her freedom. She had two more books in the works, one about aging and the other about love, both of which needed her sustained attention.

Ironing. Laundry. Could it be true? If so, that utter simplicity I remembered from a decade ago was unchanged. I imagined the small puffs of steam belching upward, the mounting piles of warm, smooth linen on the kitchen table. Did she use a modern iron with an electric cord, I wondered, or one of those cast iron ones that you heat on the stove, the kind that has no cord, yet is not cordless in the way we use that term now?

I am familiar with those irons that you heat over the gas. My ex-husband's grandmother, who witnessed at close hand many of the depredations of the twentieth century, who took in her younger brother, his health broken after ten years in the gulag for stealing a bottle of vodka on a dare, and nursed him until he died—my ex-grandmother-in-law, her nostalgia for the Stalin years palpable and intact, held on, God knows why, to several of those early twentieth-century, sharp-edged, pointed, heavy hunks of black metal.

They came in handy on the occasions, increasingly frequent around the time of Communism's collapse, when the power would go out in the capital of Soviet Georgia, leaving us in the dark sometimes for nights on end. We never knew exactly why the power failed, only that it added to the general sense of apocalypse. The night before we married, she brought out those irons, heating them on the gas, and we pressed our wedding clothes by candlelight.

I can no longer ask Alexandra Pavlovna, whom I knew as "Bobbo" (Russian for "Granny"), why she saved them. I suspect she knew their time would come around again. Or perhaps, because she'd known deprivation—she'd lost a sister to starvation in the Siege of Leningrad, then taken in the tiny, motherless girl left behind—she was incapable of throwing away a stale crust of bread, let alone perfectly serviceable household implements.

Svetlana is of course far younger than Bobbo, but she's seen plenty too. She too might have such irons stored on a high shelf, handed down, perhaps, from her mother. Her mother, who, according to the press, had been a country schoolteacher.

———

I lose myself in these musings so as not to batter myself with recriminations over the Nobel. My approach, honed over years (more than a decade now) of chronic illness, is my own blend of acceptance and denial. It is not good to dwell on what might have been: the participation in something meaningful, the inherent satisfaction, and yes, the honor and prestige, and perhaps a modest financial windfall—these could-have-beens, catalogued here from most important down to least.

Who in our culture, where celebrity equals godhood, would not want to be this close to glory? To deny this would be disingenuous. For there must be few things more miraculous to witness at close range or to live through than that instant when the light falls on something long swathed in shadow, washing it golden and bestowing worldly sense upon years of toil and obscurity. Walking backward as we do into whatever awaits, we never know whether or when this will happen. Or how. Or why.

———

All the reasons I declined: I remember them well. They were valid back then, every single one, and none of them had gone away in the meantime. Yet trying now to turn back the clock, I chased the assignment, worked my old contacts, sent off translation samples to agents and publishers once again. This was shameless, I knew, and I also knew that jumping on the bandwagon now, even if I was successful in doing so, would afford nothing like the delight that would have been mine had I simply accepted the translations when they were offered and awakened years later to the fruity, rounded tones of National Public Radio announcing Svetlana's triumph.

———————

I would soon learn that a well-known two-person team (American husband, Russian wife) had just been tapped to translate those of Alexievich's books that were still unavailable in English. This pair had already retranslated most of Russian literature; Tolstoy, Dostoyevsky, and Chekhov were only the most famous of the authors, already available in countless translations, whom they had done over.

The husband has described their methods in the press. He works from his wife's literal, line-by-line renderings. (There are conflicting reports as to whether he in fact knows Russian at all, an issue that seems to spark some defensiveness in them both.) He compares her pages with previous translations of the same work because, he says, without them, it is impossible to make sense of the crib she has provided. He cleans up what she's handed him, making it, as he put it once in a public lecture I attended, "more literary." And so we may in fact have the worst of both worlds: a translation that is excessively literal, buffed and polished by someone whose grasp of the original is weak to nonexistent.

The final product is somehow based both on previous translations of the same work and on the wife's rough version. And while this method might just work for Tolstoy, Dostoyevsky, and other titans who've been translated countless times before, it sounds an awful lot like the way generations of schoolboys got through Latin and Greek, by relying on a trot (defined as "a literal translation used illicitly in doing schoolwork"). I cannot help wondering how it will stand up when applied to the work of Alexievich: contemporary, colloquial, utterly unlike anything this pair has ever done before, and—not least important—never before put into English, ever. How will the American husband make sense of his Russian wife's avowedly perplexing take on things with no earlier renderings to shed light? This couple can do over, yes, but can they simply do?

———————

I barrel through Alexievich's books now, one after the other, all five, without surfacing in between. In all my life, I've never read so many Russian books at one go, and the more I read, the more I crave. I cling to these books; they keep me afloat through days of office work and shortness of breath. Over solitary meals and on the subway I imbibe them, in the bathroom, and in bed. Her ability to bring readers into proximity with people and situations utterly removed from their day-to-day lives—this is the real thing. For the weeks it takes me to read them, they become the point of my existence, though, objectively, what they offer has little to do with me.

For what have I in common with the mother of a veteran of the Soviet war in Afghanistan whose son returns from the war so traumatized that she procures prostitutes for him and even becomes, as she delicately puts it, his mistress for a night? Later, he does a Raskolnikov, committing a random murder with a meat cleaver borrowed from her kitchen, and where once she waited years for him to come home from war, she now travels long distances to visit him behind bars.

And what have I in common with the Soviet patriots in Alexievich's books, admirers of Stalin who, speaking into her omnipresent tape recorder, rue the passing of Communism, report that they continue each year to celebrate with gusto the anniversary of the October Revolution, then segue into tales of the beatings they endured in KGB cellars; the weeks or months they spent en route to remote prison camps, upright in jammed cattle cars with no facilities but an overflowing bucket in the corner; the loss of a wife or a father or ten to twenty years of their own life to the gulag; or, perhaps worst of all, a coerced promotion from tortured to torturer?

One man she interviews, beaten, imprisoned, and widowed by the state (which would later rehabilitate him and, posthumously, his wife), loyally bequeaths his apartment to the atrophied Communist Party twenty years after the Soviet Union is dust.

Alexievich exercises her gifts invisibly; this is what the genre imposes. The sentences are not hers, the style and the characters— not hers. Her talent lies in the way people open up to her, but there is almost nothing in the books themselves to indicate how she achieves that. What makes people spill what they spill, things they've never spilled before? Her skill at extracting truths is so tremendous that the tellers themselves become ill at ease with what they turn out to know. Some of them sue her for defamation, even as they affirm that she quoted them accurately.

There are other aspects to her artistry, secrets buried in the outtakes. How does she decide what to keep and what to omit; what makes the final cut and what ends up on the cutting room floor; how to sequence sections and speakers, how to choreograph a book? The answers to these questions also lie outside the covers of her works.

Some ask whether what Svetlana Alexievich does is art. I know only that it is almost unbearably gripping and that the true stories she draws forth and presents have far more urgency than most of the fables or fictions now being written. Each time I close one of her books, I think: yes, her critics may well be right when they say that the Nobel Prize for Literature should not have been hers. Perhaps she should have gotten the Peace Prize.

In a remark that I came across long ago and cannot source, some literary critic, Edmund Wilson, let's say (I choose him because he taught himself to read in Russian), gave three reasons why every intermediate-level Russian language student should plow through

War and Peace in the original, start to finish. It is a valuable exercise, this critic said, because Tolstoy's style, simple and clear, is accessible to someone who's been working at Russian for just a few years; because the novel's frequent interludes in "that refined French in which our grandfathers not only spoke but thought," as Tolstoy has it very early in the book, provide the weary reader with a rest from the Russian parts; and because the book is so long that by the time the reader arrives at the end, her knowledge of Russian will be greatly improved. (Protracted stretches of Russian intercut with briefer ones of French, all of this going on for a long, long time, culminating at last in a greatly improved grasp of Russian. Why, it sounds like a highly compressed account of my own life.)

Perhaps the five volumes of Alexievich are my *War and Peace*, though some say they are not Russian (because she is Belarusian) and others that they are not literature. My Alexievich marathon is the latest stage in my trek toward the mysterious heart of Russian literature, a trip I embarked on some three decades ago, boundless optimism and persistence my only cargo. Russian literature hovers forever before me, a mirage on the horizon. For years on end, it seems to get no closer, and then from time to time it expands to fill half the sky.

My Alexievich marathon signals as well one phase in my twisting writing path. I chose my writing over hers—isn't this what creative people are supposed to do, sacrificing whatever they must so as to clear space for their work? If there exists a map guiding this writing journey of mine—I imagine one of those antique charts fading out at the unexplored margins of the world, where, wreathed in flame and emitting puffs of smoke, dragons lounge and flick their tails—then here is a section of it, reader, unfolded before you now.

As the decades pass, the losses mount. No surprise there. Some version of this happens—doesn't it?—to all of us who make it to midlife.

What has taken me by surprise is that in struggling to minimize the very heaviest losses — to save myself from going under, to swim ashore — I unwittingly called down further ones. To survive, or else to slow my decline — I'll never know which — I chose the nine-to-five job and the little yellow pill, and in doing so, I sacrificed a treasure.

I had to live another ten years to find out exactly what I'd passed up. And if I'd said yes to the Midwestern publisher, agreed to translate the books, turned my back on the job, with its irresistible, indispensible remunerations and unavoidable humiliations? I would not have gotten the yellow pill, might not have been able to finish translating those books, not have lived to see where my labors led or to watch on YouTube as Svetlana delivered her acceptance speech.

This does little to assuage my regrets.

Other
Incidents in
the Precinct

2.

THAT SPRING, I went to my fourth dentist in three years.

Why did I change dentists so frequently and so frivolously? My formative years gave no indication that I would engage in such behavior. I was a model of stomatological stability in my youth, sticking with the same dentist from the time I cut my teeth until my midtwenties, remaining faithful even after I went away to college and then off to seek my fortune and back, and then off again.

It has certainly occurred to me, given my more recent inability to stick with one person, that I should give up on dentistry altogether. But I hold to the belief that regular cleanings and filled cavities are preferable to the alternative.

To answer the question, though: the first of the four dentists did his job too quickly, finishing in ten minutes and raising concerns about shoddy work. The second seemed competent enough —charming, even, until during visit number three he uttered anti-Semitic smears (too convoluted to reproduce), withdrawing his arms from my mouth and setting down his pointy tool quite deliberately, challenging me to respond. About dentist number three I had no complaints, and her office was located conveniently across the street from mine, where my workdays are spent making sense of notes verbales with the help of electronic glossaries.

But the next time dentist number three was away, so her partner saw me instead.

The partner was a small, cheerful, motherly woman from the Asian subcontinent. She looked in my mouth and said, "You clench your jaw at night. Do you wake up with a headache?"

In fact I did, and I had wondered about possible causes: Dehydration? That second glass of red wine I indulged in a few nights a week? Or maybe the first?

I knew at once that she was right about the teeth-clenching, for the pain was a band that encircled my head from one corner of my mouth to the other.

"Stress," she said reproachfully. "Is your job stressful?"

"No," I said, with a sigh. I *wished* my job would provide the occasional jolt of adrenaline.

"Do you have a difficult marriage?" Her tone was brisk now.

"I am here to have my teeth cleaned," I explained.

Impressed with her diagnostic skills and eager to change the subject, I added, "You're the fourth dentist I've been to recently, and the only one to figure out that I clench my jaw. How did you know?"

She smiled as if she'd been waiting a very long time for someone to ask precisely this.

"I've been working in this office for over twenty years," she said, glancing out at the green glass high-rise across the street. "Since the early nineties. Peacekeepers were coming through when I started here, returning from Bosnia, then Rwanda. They presented with conditions we hadn't learned about in dental school. Not decay. Not cavities. I had to study up on stress-related dental conditions. You have a horizontal line inside your cheek; that's how I know."

As I spat into the sink for the last time, she said, "Oh, there is a way to relieve the stress, you know. I call it 'doing your homework.'"

I unclipped the quilted paper bib and wiped my mouth with it.

"You need to write things down," she said. "Everybody needs to. Nobody listens any more. No one has the time. In the evening before bed, sit down and write about what happened to you during the day, whatever struck you, whatever's bothering you. Get it out. *I* do it; *my* husband doesn't listen. Writing it all down will help you stop clenching."

"When you're finished, you can hit 'delete,'" she added, after a moment.

I nodded.

She ruffled my hair. "Come back next week and I'll fit you for a night guard," she said kindly.

———

I'd been having acupuncture for back and neck pain for a few years, on and off. The condition was simply a part of life, background noise.

The place was a well-oiled machine for processing insurance claims. The staff urged me to come more and more, to get all the treatment that was coming to me. They referred me for MRIs, gave me polysyllabic diagnoses, rebuked me gently because I showed up just once a week when, they assured me, insurance would cover three times that.

The sessions lasted around an hour and a half. There were three parts: electrical muscle stimulation and heat, needles, and massage.

Doctor Ping kneaded and pounded; I moaned; she cackled.

"Very good for you!" she exclaimed. "Is good! Very, very good!"

When she finished with me, I sat up, and my face, which had been buried in a doughnut cushion designed to keep the patient's nose from being squashed against the table, sometimes ran with tears and snot.

"What wrong?" she would demand in dismay when she saw my slick, wet features.

One day I whispered, "I left my husband."

I had in fact told *him* to leave, but for Dr. Ping, I wanted things to be absolutely understandable.

"Oh . . ." she said, a look of concern coming over her face. "He not nice to you?"

I shook my head.

She furrowed her brow.

"He no change?"

Again, I shook my head.

She placed a hand on the back of my head and pressed my face into her white-coated shoulder, squashing my nose.

———————

I had seen the end looming more than a year off, seen our time running out like rope unspooling off a winch, the handle going round and round, all by itself, faster and faster, rope feeding out, out, coils uncoiled, rope unwrapped, unwound, undone, coming off, coming off, no slack left, only tension, and finally, the end of the rope.

A few weeks before things came to a head, I sat on a park bench making a list of everyone I could think of who'd been divorced two times or more. It was not a short list, but it consisted mostly of people I'd never met, like Norman Mailer and Elizabeth Taylor.

As this marriage unwound, I had a range of symptoms. The first time around, my attempts at denial and postponement had presented with constipation and various infections. This time, the symptoms were different but recognizable nonetheless as signs that the end was near.

In addition to the headaches, I had a foul taste in my mouth. I went to ear, nose, and throat specialists—four. No one could find anything wrong. In the days immediately after the split, the terrible taste intensified. Growing worse and worse, it finally peaked in a tsunami of sewage-flavored viscosity rising up from within.

Then it was gone.

———————

Here's how it happened.

In the fall of the year, on what would turn out to be the last evening of our life together, I told Tristan that we must separate, and, swearing and crying, he hurled the wine glasses against the wall, also the fancy Japanese teapot he'd given me for my birthday, the earthenware roasting pan from my mother, plus lid, and other miscellaneous crockery, leaving deep dents in the plaster, and I locked myself in the bathroom with the cell and the land line, and he rattled the doorknob and switched off the light from outside, plunging me into blackness, and the friend I reached asked if she should call the police, and, my voice quavering as I sat in the dark on the lowered toilet seat, I said, "I don't know," so she did, and I came out of the bathroom with a phone in each hand and told him that we were expecting visitors, and who they were, and the two young cops arrived and asked us to please explain why they'd been called, and when I did, adding that I would like to spend the night elsewhere, they gave me five minutes to gather my things (I asked for fifteen, but the more talkative one said, "Sorry, ma'am, that won't be possible, due to other incidents in the precinct"), and Tristan reminded me to pack my medications and the portable oxygen machine I require for my lung condition, and, sobbing, he left voice mail for his best friend: "The police are here. My wife is leaving. This is the end, truly the end," and I kissed him on the forehead and I left, flanked by the police, who wheeled my suitcase out and hailed me a cab, whose driver was relieved to learn that the police were stopping him for a fare, not a violation.

———————

I stayed away for a few weeks, Tristan moved out, and I returned. Alone now for the first time in over a decade, I felt euphoria.

Or was it mania? Distinguishing between them can be difficult. I cleaned out the closets and filed every scrap of paper. I polished both sets of silver that my aunts had left me, boiled my great-grandmother's brass candlesticks in the big soup pot to remove the wax drippings, shelved all my books by subject and author, and hired a cleaning service.

My experience of marrying and splitting, and again marrying and splitting, though regrettably vaster than that of most people, is still meager as a basis for generalization; two samples are no trend. Still, I will draw some conclusions, because what else can I do with these experiences now?

And so: I think that it's hard to say, thus far, which has given me a greater sense of well-being, divorce or marriage, for that depends on what I thirst for at any given time. But since divorce obviously cannot exist independent of marriage, and marriage is so often followed, early or late, by divorce, it can be difficult to know where precisely these feelings are coming from. This alone makes me think it's time to hop off the treadmill for good. But I've been married, then single, then married again, and now single, *again*, enough times to understand that I have nothing against marriage. It's husbands I find problematic.

When my first marriage was ending, I thought it was not possible because it had never happened to me before. When my second marriage was ending, I thought it was not possible because it had already happened once. The first time, you think you chose the wrong person; the second time, *you* are the wrong person, if only because twice now you've chosen the wrong person.

The first time, people tell you that you're attractive and you'll surely meet someone else. The second time, no one says that.

———

I am surrounded, utterly surrounded, by marriages of long standing, marriages like ancient trees, of a stability that is apparently unshakeable. My parents recently marked their sixtieth year together; my brother and sister-in-law, their thirtieth; my sister and brother-in-law, their fifteenth. My nephew has been married just over three years, but with the finely honed instinct I have for matrimonial matters that concern people other than myself, I can tell that he and his bride will hang in there and join the big kids.

I feel tiny in this old growth forest, lost. I tilt back, back, back to glimpse the treetops. The effort nearly topples me backward onto the crown of my head. Those tall trees, with all of their rings marking years and storms weathered: they seem to go on forever, up, up, into the sky.

———————

There have been other divorces in the family, but the marriages that preceded them were brief and those that followed, long. Pretty much everyone else who got divorced achieved redemption in the form of a second marriage that was fruitful and lasting.

Well, except for my Aunt Esther, who, returning home one evening in the late forties from her job as an intrepid girl reporter (this is how I think of her), found on the bedroom floor some feminine item that was not hers (a lipstick? a bobby pin? all those who might remember are dead, long dead), and when her husband, home on leave from the army base in Battle Creek, took her in his arms and told her that she was the one he *really* loved, she pulled away and made up a bed for herself on the couch, and then, early the next morning, she packed her bags and left.

Esther, at least, had the sense not to try again. Oh, she had lovers, and plenty of them, I gather. When she came to visit, she would sometimes take a hotel room instead of staying at our house, and this she did, as I learned much, much later, in order to discreetly entertain someone who lived nearby.

But she never had another husband of her own, only those of other women.

———————

And then there's Kate, who hovers in the background like Lilith, somewhere close to the Garden of Eden, barred from entry.

Eleven years old, I skipped into the living room after lunch one day, just in time to hear my father saying to a guest, "Rose was still my mother-in-law back then. She had trained as a psycho-analyst and she practiced on everyone around her, free of charge. Drove Kate crazy."

I skidded, midskip. A different mother-in-law? Click, click, click, went my little brain. That must mean a different wife. That would be Kate.

I came to a halt just behind my father's chair.

"Kate's father was heir to a department store fortune in Cleve-land and held a sinecure at the University of Chicago," he went on. "The only person in that family with a drop of human kind-ness was the sister. And she was very disturbed: absolutely bald, always wore a kerchief. Kate told me she'd pulled her hair out, down to the very last strand. She—"

At this, I must have emitted some small sound.

Too late he saw me; too late, he stopped.

I spent the rest of that long afternoon in my father's lap, soak-ing his shirtfront with my tears each time it hit me anew that he had, for a time, been married to someone who was not my mother, and then taking refuge in sleep. Over and over he tried to calm me, again and again he said that this had happened long ago, that the marriage had been childless, brief, and therefore unimportant.

———————

My father was twenty-two years old when he met Kate. A friend brought him to one of her Friday afternoon things. She held them every week at her parents' house, near campus. Boys greatly out-numbered girls at these dos, but he barely registered that fact, as he barely registered that the parties slowed, then ceased, as he and Kate started going steady, or whatever expression Chicago undergraduates used back then to domesticate and sterilize the dark mysteries of sex, reducing the whole messy, dripping bundle to something that could be briefly summarized and mentioned in mixed company.

That afternoon, he explained to eleven-year-old me that the two of them wanted very much to be alone together, but back in those days, a young man and his favorite girl couldn't do that unless they were quite, quite serious about each other. That her maiden aunt, a rather romantic lady, said they could solve the problem by telling people that they were engaged. And that then a shift occurred, exactly when, he wasn't sure, from *telling* people they were engaged to actually *being* engaged. And then married.

At the time it must have felt inevitable, in ways both good and bad. This is something I understand.

That marriage lasted just five years. The main issue was the lack of issue. He wanted children, and Kate, it seems, did not. My father went into psychoanalysis, which was all the rage at Chicago in the early fifties. When at last he mustered the nerve to tell her it was over, he had to drive a long way to see her (they were living apart, ostensibly because of his job), and on the way, he ran out of gas. That was good for several sessions.

Kate swiftly siphoned off most of the joint bank account (a modest sum, but I sense that it still rankles with my father, all these many decades later), then agreed to a divorce. Her second husband was Klaus, a refugee from Germany who had landed in Chicago somehow and obtained an advanced degree in quantum physics. Time passed, how much, I cannot say. Kate and Klaus got divorced, and she married a third time.

After this, Kate disappears from view. We have no idea if that third marriage lasted. We don't know if there were any children from the third marriage (she may have been too old by then) or with anybody else. We don't know if Kate is still living. She would be very, very old now, nearly ninety, like my parents, and how would you even trace someone whose last name has changed that many times?

———

It's been sixty years or more, but the topic of Kate still comes up from time to time. She makes a good story, and my family is full of people who love a good story, and more than anything, love repeating a good story, again, again, again.

She never met her predecessor, but my mother has her own Kate story. She brought it out again recently, one evening when we were all seated around my parents' dining table. No doubt there was a context, but who remembers these things? All I know is that I was newly single, again.

"We were at a dinner party," began my mother. "This was the late fifties. The woman sitting next to me started talking about this friend of hers, this wonderful, courageous woman." At the words "wonderful, courageous," my mother's voice grew harsh, ironic.

I locked eyes with my sister. Both of us knew where our mother was headed with this.

She pressed on. "Your dad was way at the other end of the table, so he didn't hear any of this. The woman said her friend had been divorced, and now she was going to try a second time. She was going to marry again! How brave, right? And I'm listening to this, and from the biographical details, I realize it's Kate she's talking about!"

Now my mother's tone turned downright grim. "So, I said to the woman, 'Actually, you may not know that your friend has in fact been divorced twice. My husband is her *first* ex-husband. They got divorced and then she married and divorced a second time.'"

In the telling, my mother's dinner companion was thunder-struck by the heinous deception Kate had perpetrated.

My mother tells this story with a triumphal air; she was shining light in a dark corner, striking a blow for truth. Kate was masquerading as a once-divorced woman, someone who had made a simple mistake; my mother outed her as a double divorcée, a serial screwup.

The story struck a nerve this time.

"Of course she didn't want people to know!" I exclaimed. "Why did you have to expose her? Whose business was it but her own?"

My mother looked at me, astonished.

"And," I added wearily, "I've heard that story so many times."

"I'm sorry if I bore you," said my mother, in that same harsh tone.

My sister immediately started updating the family about her mother-in-law, who had recently been in and out of the hospital, and then in again.

I'd heard all that before too, so I stood up from the table and carried my plate into the kitchen. From there, I drifted into the back bedroom.

———

I lay on the bedspread, listening to the voices rise and fall two rooms away.

For forty minutes or so, I lay there. I dozed. Then I lay there some more, wishing that somebody would come talk to me.

I washed my face in the adjoining water closet and was looking for a towel when my mother entered the bedroom, calling out my name as if searching for a small child lost in the forest.

"I'm so sorry," she said, hugging me as I emerged, face dripping. "How thoughtless of me. Why didn't somebody kick me under the table?"

We sat on the edge of the bed as darkness fell.

"I'm thinking about my old friend Pearl," she said finally.

My mother was twelve when she met Pearl. A few years older than my mother, Pearl went on to become a modern dancer and choreographer of distinction. She married twice, the second time in her forties. As she segued inexorably from her first husband, a man with no visible means of support whose friends believed him to be a Soviet agent, to her second, the actor who played the title role in the very first James Bond picture, *Dr. No* (and also in *Hamlet*), she sat at my parents' kitchen table, weeping and saying over and over, "What should I do? What should I do?"

A year or two later, having extricated herself from the marriage to the putative spy and wedded Dr. No, she explained tranquilly, "People's needs change."

"People's needs change," my mother now quoted Pearl, with a pensive air. Never divorced herself, this is how my mother explains the marriages that shatter, collapse, or run out of gas. It's touching. It is.

I assumed the blank look I keep for when I've heard the story before. I'd first heard about Pearl and her changing needs seventeen years back, when my *first* marriage ended.

Aleksandr, my first husband, remarried and became a father just shy of fifty. If ever his children hear of me, I will be their Kate, forever hovering just outside Eden's gate. Tristan, quite a bit younger, has a good ten years yet to pull off the same thing, making me into Kate for yet another set of children.

I've been hearing the story of Kate nearly my whole life long. The story of Kate is now becoming the story of me.

The significance of Kate, the subtext of Kate, from our family's standpoint, which is the standpoint of my father, who got it right with my mother, the second time around, has always been that if you make a mistake, you will be granted another chance. That the consequences of a single mistake are not necessarily devastating. From our collective, familial point of view, Kate stands in for optimism.

But what is the meaning of Kate from the standpoint of Kate? What did she tell herself as she traipsed from one marriage to the next? That it was always the husband's fault? That point of view must certainly have been a tempting one to espouse. And what if it really and truly was? The other person's fault, I mean. Where, precisely, does truth bleed into self-justification?

I have no answers. The self-help books, to which I have turned whenever I find myself in a marriage that is nearing its end time, state categorically that it takes two to fail. There is always, they say, responsibility enough to go around.

If you discover that your husband, who will turn out to have been your first, has advertised for a woman on the Internet, do you stay? If you both wanted children, discussed the matter at length before marrying, and then he no longer does, and he cannot explain this shift, do you stay? Do you stay if you see in him a vast and terrifying anger that must certainly have something to do with you but also predates you, an anger that on most days flows noiselessly underground but also surfaces from time to time, roaring, foaming, and spreading swiftly outward in all directions like a river filling its flood plain, until it seems certain that everything you have will be swept away?

If you learn that for the better part of a year your next husband slept with someone else, both at her place (he said he was meeting a friend, which was not an unadulterated lie), and at yours (you were at work), and also, in warm weather, on top of a high, flat boulder in the park across the street (it was past midnight and you were at home, in bed, in dreamland, alone), what do you do? What do you do if that husband, your second, is enrolled in graduate school for a year, then another, then another, the missed deadlines adding up finally to more than a decade, and his taste in clothing, in shoes, in restaurants, in wine and whiskey and hand-crafted pipes from Italy and tobacco also spiral upward during this time, threatening to outstrip your income, which is designed to support a family of four? What do you do?

Are there marriages that are easier than this? Less troubled? Marriages where things like this don't happen? And, if so, where might you find one?

Recognizing that nothing is perfect, and marriage least of all, believing that you should tough it out, work at it and see if things get better, how much should you accept?

How much can you stand? When do you eject?

The books all say that since a couple is a system, subtle adjustments in *your* behavior will make these problems fade. Which is not the same as saying the problems are somehow your fault. No. Not the same as saying: They are.

———

I was supposed to learn something from the first time, that was what I thought, fashion some sort of template that I could then whip out and apply to a second marriage, should one come to pass, and presto, I would trace the right shape this time and draw the lines straight. I had always gotten decent grades. I just needed to master the material, somewhat reshuffled perhaps, and sit for a makeup.

But no. It was no simple redo. It turns out that each time is unique. Although both times there was nothing to do finally but crawl out of the wreckage, check for scratches and broken bones, and walk slowly away, looking back for a time, trying to figure out what happened, and why. Continuing all the while to walk away, slowly away.

———————

Oh, Kate, I think now: your friend at the dinner party was right, fifty-odd years ago. It *was* brave of you, awfully brave, maybe even foolhardy: the second time, the third time, the fourth time, if there was a fourth time that we never heard about, *every* time, however many times there eventually were, and maybe the first time too.

Oh, Kate, how did you keep on doing it?

And why?

———————

Some months after what I now think of as the night of the flying crockery, springtime came circling around once more, and again it was time to have my teeth cleaned. (Amid the turmoil of life, I had let a year go by between appointments.)

The dentist looked in my mouth and emerged beaming. In one graceful movement, she stripped off her latex elbow gloves and dropped them in the medical waste bin.

"You've stopped clenching," she announced. "The line on your cheek is gone. Are things going well?"

I smiled mysteriously.

"Are you doing your homework?" she asked. "Writing it all down?"

"A little bit. Not every day, though," I said apologetically.

Nor did I hit delete, as she had said to do. I didn't mention that part.

"Well," she said, patting my shoulder, "whatever you're doing, keep on doing it."

———————

I have wondered, in the months since this exchange, what it might mean to keep on doing what I'm doing. Marry and divorce another time? Or simply continue basking in solitude?

I had told the dentist nothing of the recent changes in my life, so I could not ask her what she meant; she herself would not know.

Of all the mutually incompatible, contradictory things I had done at various times, which ones should I continue doing, and from which of them should I desist?

The dentist could not point the way; no one can.

Acknowledgments

Thanks to Cheryl M. Kaplan, Elizabeth Kostova, Slava Paperno, and Burton Shulman, first readers of the full manuscript; Dominique Lavoie, Richard Ryan, Ileana Santamaria, Lynn Visson, Jesse Wolfson, and Paul Wolfson, first readers of various sections of it; Meghan Daum and her students in the nonfiction MFA program at the University of Iowa, for finding it; Francine Prose, for teaching me to ponder every comma; Jill Dearman and Alan Schwarz, for advice that bore fruit; Leonid Fridman, for words of encouragement back in the nineties; Yevsey Tseytlin, whose book Долгие беседы в ожидании счастливой смерти (Long conversations in anticipation of a joyous death), for which no English translation is yet available, provided inspiration for parts of "The Book of Disaster"; Dovid Katz, scholar of Yiddish language and literature, who also provided inspiration for part of "The Book of Disaster"; Victoria Pryor of Arcadia Literary Agency, Charlie Graeber, and Stephanie Picinic for generosity with their time and expertise; and Carolyn Brown, Gemma de Choisy, and all the hardworking people at the University of Iowa Press, for pretty much everything.

Grateful acknowledgement is made to the *New School Chapbook Series,* and to the journals (both online and print) and anthologies listed below, where most of the sections appeared previously, in somewhat different form and, in some cases, under different titles.

The Alembic, Bellingham Review, Columbia: A Journal of Literature and Art, Confrontation, The Fourth River, Gettysburg

Review, North Atlantic Review, North Dakota Quarterly, Poetry Daily, The Rambler, The Rumpus, The Sun, Superstition Review, Zyzzyva.

"Losing the Nobel" is included in *Five Ways of Being a Painting and Other Essays: The Winners of the Third Notting Hill Editions Essay Prize* (London: Notting Hill Editions, 2017); "The Husband Method" (under the title "In Love with Russian") is included in *Crossing Borders, Stories and Essays About Translation*, ed. Lynne Sharon Schwartz (New York: Seven Stories Press, 2017); "For Single Women Working as Train Conductors" is included (in Swedish translation) in *Gränslös: Toliga, allvarliga och annorlunda berättelser om resor* (Without borders: Comical, serious and wacky tales of travel), vol. 2 (Stockholm: Sandnejlika Förlag, 2016).

IOWA PRIZE FOR LITERARY NONFICTION

———————

2016
*China Lake: A Journey into the Contradicted
Heart of a Global Climate Catastrophe*
by Barret Baumgart

2017
For Single Mothers Working as Train Conductors
by Laura Esther Wolfson